Frank J. Hannon.

Under the Prophet in Utah

The National Menace of a Political Priestcraft

BY

FRANK J. CANNON

Formerly United States Senator from Utah

AND

HARVEY J. O'HIGGINS

Author

"The Smoke-Eaters," "Don-a-Dreams," etc.

THE C. M. CLARK PUBLISHING CO.

BOSTON, MASSACHUSETTS

1911

CONTENTS

NOTE

When Harvey J. O'Higgins was in Denver, in the
spring of 1910, working with Judge Ben B. Lindsey
on the manuscript of "The Beast and the Jungle,"
for *Everybody's Magazine*, he met the Hon. Frank J.
Cannon, formerly United States Senator from Utah,
and heard from him the story of the betrayal of Utah
by the present leaders of the Mormon Church. This
story the editor of *Everybody's Magazine* commis-
sioned Messrs. Cannon and O'Higgins to write. They
worked on it for a year, verifying every detail of it
from government reports, controversial pamphlets,
Mormon books of propaganda, and the newspaper
files of current record. It ran through nine numbers
of the magazine, and not so much as a successful
contradiction was ever made of one of the innumerable
incidents or accusations that it contains. It is here
published in book form at somewhat greater length
than the magazine could print it. It is a joint work,
but the autobiographic "I" has been used throughout, because it is Mr. Cannon's personal narrative
of his personal experience.

INTRODUCTION

This is the story of what has been called "the great American despotism."

It is the story of the establishment of an absolute throne and dynasty by one American citizen over a half-million others.

And it is the story of the amazing reign of this one man, Joseph F. Smith, the Mormon Prophet, a religious fanatic of bitter mind, who claims that he has been divinely ordained to exercise the awful authority of God on earth over all the affairs of all mankind, and who plays the anointed despot in Utah and the surrounding states as cruelly as a Sultan and more securely than any Czar.

To him the Mormon people pay a yearly tribute of more than two million dollars in tithes; and he uses that income, to his own ends, without an accounting. He is president of the Utah branch of the sugar trust, and of the local incorporations of the salt trust; and he supports the exactions of monopoly by his financial absolutism, while he defends them from competition by his religious power of interdict and excommunication. He is president of a system of "company stores," from which the faithful buy their merchandise; of a wagon and machine company from which the Mormon farmers purchase their vehicles and implements; of life-insurance and fire-insurance companies, of banking institutions, of a railroad, of a knitting company, of newspapers, which the Mormon people are required by their Church to patronize, and through which they are exploited, commercially and financially, for the sole profit of the sovereign of Utah and his religious court.

He is the political Boss of the state, delivering

9

the votes of his people by revelation of the Will of God, practically appointing the United States Senators from Utah—as he practically appoints the marshals, district attorneys, judges, legislators, officers and administrators of law throughout his "Kingdom of God on Earth"—and ruling the non-Mormons of Utah, as he rules his own people, by virtue of his political and financial partnership with the great "business interests" that govern and exploit this nation, and his Kingdom, for their own gain, and his.

He lives, like the Grand Turk, openly with five wives, against the temporal law of the state, against the spiritual law of his Kingdom, and in violation of his own solemn covenant to the country—which he gave in 1890, in order to obtain amnesty for himself from criminal prosecution and to help Utah obtain the powers of statehood which he has since usurped. He secretly preaches a proscribed doctrine of polygamy as necessary to salvation; he publicly denies his own teaching, so that he may escape responsibility for the sufferings of the "plural wives" and their unfortunate children, who have been betrayed by the authority of his dogma. And these women, by the hundreds, seduced into clandestine marriage relations with polygamous elders of the Church, unable to claim their husbands—even in some cases disowning their children and teaching these children to deny their parents—are suffering a pitiful self-immolation as martyrs to the religious barbarism of his rule.

Demanding unquestioning obedience in all things, as the "mouthpiece of the Lord," and "sole vicegerent of God on Earth," he enforces his demands by his religious, political and financial control of the faith, the votes and the property of his fellow-citizens. He is at once—as the details of this story show—"the modern 'money king,' the absolute political Czar, the social despot and the infallible Pope of his Kingdom."

Ex-Senator Cannon not only exposes but accounts for and explains the conditions that have made the Church-controlled government of Utah less free, less of a democracy, a greater tyranny and more of a disgrace to the nation than ever the corporation rule of Colorado was in the darkest period of the Cripple Creek labor war. He shows the enemies of the republic encouraging and profiting by the shame of Utah as they supported and made gain of Colorado's past disgrace. He shows the piratical "Interests," at Washington, sustaining, and sustained by, the misgovernment of Utah, in their campaign of national pillage. He shows that the condition of Utah today is not merely a local problem; that it affects and concerns the people of the whole country; that it can only be cured with their aid.

The outside world has waited many years to hear the truth about the Mormons; here it is—told with sympathy, with affection, by a man who steadfastly defended and fought for the Mormon people when their present leaders were keeping themselves carefully inconspicuous. The Mormon system of religious communism has long been known as one of the most interesting social experiments of modern civilization; here is an intimate study of it, not only in its success but in the failure that has come upon it from the selfish ambitions of its leaders. The power of the Mormon hierarchy has been the theme of much imaginative fiction; but here is a story of church tyranny and misgovernment in the name of God, that outrages the credibilities of art. That such a story could come out of modern America—that such conditions could be possible in the democracy today—is an amazement that staggers belief.

11

II

Hon. Frank J. Cannon is the son of George Q. Cannon of Utah, who was First Councillor of the Mormon Church from 1880 to 1901. After the death of Brigham Young, George Q. Cannon's diplomacy saved the Mormon communism from destruction by the United States government. It was his influence that lifted the curse of polygamy from the Mormon faith. Under his leadership Utah obtained the right of statehood; and his financial policies were establishing the Mormon people in industrial prosperity when he died.

In all these achievements the son shared with his father, and in some of them—notably in the obtaining of Utah's statehood—he had even a larger part than George Q. Cannon himself. When the Mormon communities, in 1888, were being crushed by proscription and confiscation and the righteous bigotries of Federal officials, Frank J. Cannon went to Washington, alone —almost from the doors of a Federal prison—and, by the eloquence of his plea for his people, obtained from President Cleveland a mercy for the Mormons that all the diplomacies of the Church's politicians had been unable to procure. Again, in 1890, when the Mormons were threatened with a general disfranchisement by means of a test oath, he returned to Washington and saved them, with the aid of James G. Blaine, on the promise that the doctrine and practice of polygamy were to be abandoned by the Mormon Church; and he assisted in the promulgation and acceptance of the famous "manifesto" of 1890, by which the Mormon Prophet, as the result of a "divine revelation," withdrew the doctrine of polygamy from the practice of the faith.

He organized the Republican party in Utah, and led it in the first campaigns that divided the people of the territory on the lines of national issues and

freed them from the factions of a religious dispute.
He delivered to Washington the pledges of the Mormon leaders, by which the emancipation of their people
from hierarchical domination was promised and the
right of statehood finally obtained. He was elected
the first United States Senator from Utah, against
the unwilling candidacy of his own father, when the
intrigues of the Mormon priests pitted the father
against the son and violated the Church's promise
of non-interference in politics almost as soon as it
had been given.

It was his voice, in the Senate, that helped to re-
awaken the national conscience to the crimes of
Spanish rule in Cuba, when the "financial interests"
of this country were holding the government back
from any interference in Cuban affairs. He was one
of the leaders in Washington of the first ill-fated
"Insurgent Republican" movement against the control of the Republican party by these same piratical
"interests;" and he was the only Republican Senator
who stood to oppose them by voting against the
iniquitous Dingley tariff bill of 1897. He delivered
the speech of defiance at the Republican national
convention of 1896, when four "Silver Republican"
Senators led their delegations out of that convention
in revolt. And by all these acts of independence
he put himself in opposition to the politicians of the
Mormon Church, who were allying themselves with
Hanna and Aldrich, the sugar trust, the railroad lobby,
and the whole financial and commercial Plunderbund
in politics that has since come to be called "The
System."

He returned to Utah to prevent the sale of a United
States Senatorship by the Mormon Church; and,
though he was himself defeated for re-election, he
helped to hold the Utah legislature in a deadlock that
prevented the selection of a successor to his seat. He
fought to compel the leaders of the Church to fulfil

the pledges which they had authorized him to give
in Washington when statehood was being obtained.
After his father's death, when these pledges began
to be openly violated, he directed his attack particularly against Joseph F. Smith, the new President of
the Church, who was principally responsible for the
Church's breach of public faith.   Through the col-
umns of the *Salt Lake Tribune* he exposed the treason-
able return to the practice of polygamy which Joseph
F. Smith had secretly authorized and encouraged.
He opposed the election of Apostle Reed Smoot to
the United States Senate, as a violation of the statehood pledges.   He criticized the financial absolutism
of the Mormon Prophet, which Smith was establishing
in partnership with "the Plunderbund."   He was
finally excommunicated and ostracized, by his father's
successors in power, for championing the political and
social liberties of the Mormon people whom he had
helped to save from destruction and whose statehood
sovereignty he had so largely obtained.

When the partnership of the Church and "the
Interests" prevented the expulsion of Apostle Smoot
from the Senate, Senator Cannon withdrew from
Utah, convinced that nothing could be done for the
Mormons so long as the national administration
sustained the sovereignty of the Mormon kingdom
as a co-ordinate power in this Republic.   For the
last few years he has been a newspaper editor in
Denver, Colorado—on the *Denver Times* and the
Rocky Mountain News—helping the reform movement
in Colorado against the corporation control of that
state, and waiting for the opportunity to renew his
long fight for the Mormon people.

In the following narrative he returns to that fight.
In fulfilment of a promise made before he left Utah—
and seeing now, in the new "insurgency," the hope
of freeing Utah from slavery to "the System"—he
here addresses himself to the task of exposing the

14

treasons and tyrannies of the Mormon Prophet and the consequent miseries among his people.

In the course of his exposition, he gives a most remarkable picture of the Mormon people, patient, meek, and virtuous, "as gentle as the Quakers, as staunch as the Jews." He introduces the world for the first time to the conclaves of the Mormon ecclesiasts, explains the simplicity of some of them, the bitterness of others, the sincerity of almost all—illuminating the dark places of Church control with the understanding of a sympathetic experience, and bringing out the virtues of the Mormon system as impartially as he exposes its faults. He traces the degradation of its communism, step by step and incident by incident, from its success as a sort of religious socialism administered for the common good to its present failure as a hierarchical capitalism governed for the benefit of its modern "Prophet of Mammon" at the expense of the liberty, the happiness, and even the prosperity, of its victims.

For the first time in the history of the Mormon Church, there has arrived a man who has the knowledge and the inclination to explain it.

He does this fearlessly, as a duty, and without any apologies, as a public right. "He is not, and never has been an official member of the Church, in any sense or form," Joseph F. Smith, as President of the Church, testified concerning him, at Washington in 1904; and though this statement is one of the inspired Prophet's characteristic perversions of the truth, it covers the fact that Senator Cannon has always opposed the official tyrannies of the hierarchs. The present Mormon leaders accepted his aid in freeing Utah, well aware of his independence. They profited by his success with a more or less doubtful gratitude. They betrayed him promptly—as they betrayed the nation and their own followers—as soon as they found themselves in a position safely to betray. In this

15

book he merely continues an independence which he has always maintained, and replies to secret and personal treason with a public criticism, to which he has never hesitated to resort.

He begins his story with the year 1888, and devotes the first chapters to a depiction of the miseries of the Mormon people in the unhappy days of persecution. He continues with the private details of the confidential negotiations in Washington and the secret conferences in Salt Lake City by which the Mormons were saved. He gives the truth about the political intrigues that accompanied the grant of Utah's statehood, and he relates, pledge by pledge, the covenants then given by the Mormon leaders to the nation and since treasonably violated and repudiated by them. He explains the progress of this repudiation with an intimate "inside" knowledge of facts which the Mormon leaders now deny. And he exposes the horror of conditions in Utah today as no other man in America could expose them—for his life has been spent in combating the influences of which these conditions are the result; and he understands the present situation as a doctor understands the last stages of a disease which he has been for years vainly endeavoring to check.

But aside from all this—aside from his exposure of the Mormon despotism, his study of the degradation of a modern community, or his secret history of the Church's dark policies in "sacred places"—he relates a story that is full of the most astonishing curiosities of human character and of dramatic situations that are almost mediæval in their religious aspects. He goes from interviews with Cleveland or Blaine to discuss American politics with men who believe themselves in direct communication with God—who talk and act like the patriarchs of the Old Testament—who accept their own thoughts as the inspiration of the Holy Ghost, and deliver their personal decisions, reverently, as the Will of the Lord. He shows men and women ready to suffer any martyrdom in defence of a doctrine of polygamy that is a continual unhappiness and cross upon them. He depicts the social life of the most peculiar sect that has ever lived in a Western civilization. He writes—unconsciously, and for the first time that it has ever been written— the naive, colossal drama of modern Mormonism.

H. J. O'H.

FOREWORD

On the fourth day of January, 1896, the territory of Utah was admitted to statehood, and the proscribed among its people were freed to the liberties of American citizenship, upon the solemn covenant of the leaders of the Mormon Church that they and their followers would live, thereafter, according to the laws and institutions of the nation of which they were allowed to become a part. And that gracious settlement of upwards of forty years of conflict was negotiated through responsible mediators, was endorsed by the good faith of the non-Mormons of Utah, and was sealed by a treaty convention in which the high contracting parties were the American Republic and the "Kingdom of God on Earth."

I propose, in this narrative, to show that the leaders of the Mormon Church have broken their covenant to the nation; that they have abused the confidence of the Gentiles of Utah and betrayed the trust of the people under their power, by using that power to prevent the state of Utah from becoming what it had engaged to become. I propose to show that the people of Utah, upraised to freedom by the magnanimity of the nation, are being made to appear traitorous to the generosity that saved them; that

the Mormons of Utah are being falsely misled
into the peculiar dangers from which they
thought they had forever escaped; that the
unity, the solidarity, the loyalty of these
fervent people is being turned as a weapon
of offence against the whole country, for the
greater profit of the leaders and the aggran-
dizement of their power. I undertake, in
fact, in this narrative, to expose and to demon-
strate what I do believe to be one of the most
direful conspiracies of treachery in the history
of the United States.

Not that I have anything in my heart
against the Mormon people! Heaven forbid!
I know them to be great in their virtues,
wholesome in their relations, capable of an
heroic fortitude, living by the tenderest sentiments of fraternity, as gentle as the Quakers,
as staunch as the Jews. I think of them as
a man among strangers thinks of the dearness
of his home. I am bound to them in affection by all the ties of life. The smiles of
neighborliness, the greetings of friends, all
the familiar devotion of brothers and sisters,
the love of the parents who held me in their
arms—by these I know them as my own
people, and by these I love them as a good
people, as a strong people, as a people worthy
to be strong and fit to be loved.

But it is even through their virtue and by
their very strength that they are being betrayed. A human devotion—the like of

which has rarely lived among the citizens of any modern state—is being directed as an instrument of subjugation against others and held as a means of oppression upon the Mormons themselves. Noble when they were weak, they are being led to ignoble purpose now that they have become strong. Praying for justice when they had no power, now that they have gained power it is being abused to ends of injustice. Their leaders, reaching for the fleshpots for which these simple-hearted devotees have never sighed, have allied themselves with all the predaceous "interests" of the country and now use the superhuman power of a religious tyranny to increase the dividends of a national plunder.

In the long years of misery when the Mormons of Utah were proscribed and hunted, because they refused to abandon what was to them, at that time, a divine revelation and a confirmed article of faith, I sat many times in the gallery of the Senate in Washington, and heard discussed new measures of destruction against these victims of their own fidelity, and felt the dome above me impending like a brazen weight of national resentment upon all our heads. When, a few years later, I stood before the President's desk in the Senate chamber, to take my oath of office as the representative of the freed people of Utah in the councils of the nation, I raised my eyes to my old seat of terror in

21

the gallery, and pledged myself, in that remembrance, never to vote nor speak for anything but the largest measure of justice that my soul was big enough to comprehend. By such engagement I write now, bound in a double debt of obligation to the nation whose magnanimity then saved us and to the people whom I humbly helped to save.

FRANK J. CANNON.

Under the Prophet in Utah

CHAPTER I

IN THE DAYS OF THE RAID

About ten o'clock one night in the spring of 1888, I set out secretly, from Salt Lake City, on a nine-mile drive to Bountiful, to meet my father, who was concealed "on the underground," among friends; and that night drive, with its haste and its apprehension, was so of a piece with the times, that I can hardly separate it from them in my memory. We were all being carried along in an uncontrollable sweep of tragic events. In a sort of blindness, like the night, unable to see the nearest fork of the road ahead of us, we were being driven to a future that held we knew not what.

I was with my brother Abraham (soon to become an apostle of the Mormon Church), who had himself been in prison and was still in danger of arrest. And there is something typical of those days in the recollection I have of him in the carriage: silent, self-contained, and—when he talked—discussing trivialities in the most calm way in the world. The whole district was picketed with deputy marshals; we did not know that we were not being followed; we had always the sense of evading patrols in an enemy's country. But this feeling was so old with us that it had become a thing of no regard.

There was something even more typical in the personality of our driver—a giant of a man named Charles Wilcken—a veteran of the German army who had been decorated with the Iron Cross for bravery on the field of battle. He had come to Utah with General Johnston's forces in 1858, and had left the military service to attach himself to Brigham Young. After Young's death, my father had succeeded to the first place in his affections. He was an elder of the Church; he had been an aristocrat in his own country; but he forgot his every personal interest in his loyalty to his leaders, and he stood at all times ready to defend them with his life—as a hundred thousand others did!—for, though the Mormons did not resist the processes of law for themselves, except by evasion, they were prepared to protect their leaders, if necessary, by force of arms.

With Wilcken holding the reins on a pair of fast horses at full speed, we whirled past the old adobe wall (which the Mormons had

24

built to defend their city from the Indians) and came out into the purple night of Utah, with its frosty starlight and its black hills— a desert night, a mountain night, a night so vast in its height of space and breadth of distance that it seemed natural it should inspire the people that breathed it with freedom's ideals of freedom and all the sublimities of an eternal faith. And those people—!

A more despairing situation than theirs, at that hour, has never been faced by an American community. Practically every Mormon man of any distinction was in prison, or had just served his term, or had escaped into exile. Hundreds of Mormon women had left their homes and their children to flee from the officers of law; many had been behind prison bars for refusing to answer the questions put to them in court; more were concealed, like outlaws, in the houses of friends. Husbands and wives, separated by the necessities of flight, had died apart, miserably. Old men were coming out of prison, broken in health. A young plural wife whom I knew—a mere girl, of good breeding, of gentle life—seeking refuge in the mountains to save her husband from a charge of "unlawful cohabitation," had had her infant die in her arms on the road; and she had been compelled to bury the child, wrapped in her shawl, under a rock, in a grave that

25

she scratched in the soil with a stick. In our day! In a civilized state!

By Act of Congress, all the church property in excess of $50,000 had been seized by the United States marshal, and the community faced the total loss of its common fund. Because of some evasions that had been attempted by the Church authorities—and the suspicion of more such—the marshal had taken everything that he could in any way assume to belong to the Church. Among the Mormons, there was an unconquerable spirit of sanctified lawlessness, and, among the non-Mormons, an equally indomitable determination to vindicate the law. Both were, for the most part, sincere. Both were resolute. And both were standing in fear of a fatal conflict, which any act of violence might begin.

Moreover, the Mormons were being slowly but surely deprived of all civil rights. All polygamists had been disfranchised by the bill of 1882, and all the women of Utah by the bill of 1887. The Governor of the territory was appointed by Federal authority, so was the marshal, so were the judges, so were the United States Commissioners who had co-ordinate jurisdiction with magistrates and justices of the peace, so were the Election Commissioners. But the Mormons still controlled the legislature, and though the Governor could veto all legislation he could initiate none. For this reason it had been frequently proposed that the President should appoint a Legislative Council to take the place of the elected legislature; and bills were being talked of in Congress to effect a complete disfranchisement of the whole body of the Mormon people by means of a test oath.

I did not then believe, and I do not now, that the practice of polygamy was a thing which the American nation could condone. But I knew that our people believed in it as a practice ordained, by a revelation from God, for the salvation of the world. It was to them an article of faith as sacred as any for which the martyrs of any religion ever died; and it seemed that the nation, in its resolve to vindicate the supremacy of civil government, was determined to put them to the point of martyrdom.

It was with this prospect before us that we drove, that night, up the Salt Lake valley, across a corner of the desert, to the little town of Bountiful; and as soon as we arrived among the houses of the settlement, a man stepped out into the road, from the shadows, and stopped us. Wilcken spoke to him. He recognized us, and let us pass. As we turned into the farm where my father was concealed, I saw men lurking here and there, on guard, about the grounds. The house was an old-fashioned adobe farm-house; the windows were all dark; we entered through the kitchen. And I entered, let me say, with the sense that I was about to come before one of the most able among men.

To those who knew George Q. Cannon I do not need to justify that feeling. He was the man in the hands of whose sagacity the fate of the Mormons at that moment lay. He was the First Councillor of the Church, and had been so for years. For ten years in Congress, he had fought and defeated the proscriptive legislation that had been attempted against his people; and Senator Hoar had said of him, "No man in Congress ever served a territory more ably." He had been the intimate friend of Randall and Blaine. As a missionary in England he had impressed Dickens, who wrote of him in "An Uncommercial Traveller." The Hon. James Bryce had said of him: "He was one of the ablest Americans I ever met."

An Englishman, well-educated, a linguist, an impressive orator, a persuasive writer, he had lived a life that was one long incredible adventure of romance and almost miraculous achievement. As a youth he had been sent by the Mormon leaders to California to wash out gold for the struggling community; and he had sent back to Utah all the proceeds of his labor, living himself upon the crudest necessaries of life. As a young man he had gone as a Mormon missionary to the Hawaiian Islands, and finding himself unable to convert the whites he had gone among the natives—starving, a ragged wanderer—and by simple force of personality he had made himself a power among them; so that in later years Napella, the famous native leader, journeyed to Utah to consult with him upon the affairs of that distressed state, and Queen Liluokalani, deposed and in exile, appealed to him for advice. He had edited and published a Mormon newspaper in San Francisco; and he had long successfully directed the affairs of the publishing house in Salt Lake City which he owned. He was a railroad builder, a banker, a developer of mines, a financier of a score of interests. He combined the activities of a statesman, a missionary, and a man of business, and seemed equally successful in all.

But none of these things—nor all of them—contained the total of the man himself. He was greater than his work. He achieved by the force of a personality that was more impressive than its achievements. If he had been royalty, he could not have been surrounded with a greater deference than he commanded among our people. A feeling of responsibility for those dependent on him, such as a king might feel, added to a sense of divine guidance that gave him the dignity of inspiration, had made him majestical in his simple presence; and even among those who laughed at divine inspiration and scorned

29

Mormonism as the Uitlander scorned the faith of the Boer, his sagacity and his diplomacy and his power to read and handle men made him as fearfully admired as any Oom Paul in the Transvaal.

When I entered the low-ceilinged, lamplit room in which he sat, he rose to meet me, and all rose with him, like a court. He embraced me without effusion, looking at me silently with his wise blue eyes that always seemed to read in my face—and to check up in his valuation of me—whatever I had become in my absence from his regard.

He had a countenance that at no time bore any of the marks of the passions of men; and it showed, now, no shadow of the tribulations of that troubled day. His forehead was unworried. His eyes betrayed none of the anxieties with which his mind must have been busied. His expression was one of resolute stern contentment with all things— carrying the composure of spirit which he wished his people to have. If I had been agitated by the urgency of his summons to me, and he had wished to allay my anxiety at once, the sight of his face, as he looked at me, would have been reassurance enough.

At a characteristic motion of the hand from him, the others left us. We sat down in the "horse-hair" chairs of a well-to-do farmer's parlor—furnished in black walnut, with the usual organ against one wall, and the usual marble-topped bureau against the other. I remember the "store" carpet, the mortuary hair-wreaths on the walls, the walnut-framed lithographs of the Church authorities and of the angel Moroni with "the gold plates;" and none of these seem ludicrous to me to remember. They express, to me, in the recollection, some of the homely and devout simplicity of the people whose community life this man was to save.

He talked a few minutes, affectionately, about family matters, and then—straightening his shoulders to the burden of more gravity—he said: "I have sent for you, my son, to see if you cannot find some way to help us in our difficulties. I have made it a matter of prayer, and I have been led to urge you to activity. You have never performed a Mission for the Church, and I have sometimes wondered if you cared anything about your religion. You have never obeyed the celestial covenant, and you have kept yourself aloof from the duties of the priesthood, but it may have been a providential overruling. I have talked with some of the brethren, and we feel that if relief does not soon appear, our community will be scattered and the great work crushed. The Lord can rescue us, but we must put forth our own efforts. Can you see any light?"

I replied that I had already been in Washington twice, on my own initiative, conferring with some of his Congressional friends. "I am still," I said, "of the opinion I expressed to you and President Taylor four years ago. Plural marriage must be abandoned or our friends in Washington will not defend us."

Four years before, when I had offered that opinion, President Taylor had cried out: "No! Plural marriage is the will of God! It's apostasy to question it!" And I paused now with the expectation that my father would say something of this sort. But, as I was afterwards to observe, it was part of his diplomacy, in conference, to pass the obvious opportunity of replying, and to remain silent when he was expected to speak, so that he might not be in the position of following the lead of his opponent's argument, but rather, by waiting his own time, be able to direct the conversation to his own purposes. He listened to me, silently, his eyes fixed on my face.

"Senator Vest of Missouri," I went on, "has always been a strong opponent of what he considered unconstitutional legislation against us, but he tells me he'll no longer oppose proscription if we continue in an attitude of defiance. He says you're putting yourselves beyond assistance, by organized rebellion against the administration of the statutes.'" And I continued with instances of others among his friends who had spoken to the same purpose.

When I had done, he took what I had said with a gesture that at once accepted and for the moment dismissed it; and he proceeded to a larger consideration of the situation, in words which I cannot pretend to recall, but to an effect which I wish to outline—because it not only accounts for the preservation of the Mormon people from all their dangers, but contains a reason why the world might have wished to see them preserved.

The Mormons at this time had never written a line on social reform—except as the so-called "revelations" established a new social order—but they had practised whole volumes. Their community was founded on the three principles of co-operation, contribution, and arbitration. By co-operation of effort they had realized that dream of the Socialists, "equality of opportunity"—not equality of individual capacity, which the accidents of nature prevent, but an equal opportunity for each individual to develop himself to the last reach of his power. By contribution—by requiring each man to give one-tenth of his income to a common fund—they had attained the desired end of modern civilization, the abolition of poverty, and had adjusted the straps of the community burden to the strength of the individual to bear it. By arbitration, they had effected the settlement of every dispute of every kind without litigation; for their High Councils decided all sorts of personal or neighborhood disputes without expense of money to the disputants. The "storehouse of the Lord" had been kept open to fill every need of the poor among "God's people," and opportunities for self-help had been created out of the common fund, so that neither unwilling idleness nor privation might mar the growth of the community or the progress of the individual.

But Joseph Smith had gone further. Daring to believe himself the earthly representative of Omnipotence, whose duty it was to see that all had the rights to which he thought them entitled, and assuming that a woman's chief right was that of wifehood and maternity, he had instituted the practice of plural marriage, as a "Prophet of God," on the authority of a direct revelation from the Almighty. It was upon this rock that the whole enterprise, the whole experiment in religious communism, now threatened to split. Not that polygamy was so large an incident in the life of the community—for only a small proportion of the Mormons were living in plural marriage. And not that this practice was the cardinal sin of Mormonism—for among intelligent men, then as now, the great objection to the Church was its assumption of a divine authority to hold the "temporal power," to dictate in politics, to command action and to acquit of responsibility. But polygamy was the offence against civilization

34

which the opponents of Mormonism could always cite in order to direct against the Church the concentrated antagonism of the governments of the Western world. And my father, in authorizing me to proceed to Washington as a sort of ambassador of the Church, evidently wished to impress upon me the larger importance of the value of the social experiment which the Mormons had, to this time, so successfully advanced.

"It would be a cruel waste of human effort," he said, "if, after having attained comfort in these valleys—established our schools of art and science—developed our country and founded our industries—we should now be destroyed as a community, and the value of our experience lost to the world. We have a *right* to survive. We have a *duty* to survive. It would be to the profit of the nation that we *should* survive."

But in order to survive, it was necessary to obtain some immediate mitigation of the enforcement of the laws against us. The manner in which they were being enforced was making compromise impossible, and the men who administered them stood in the way of getting a favorable hearing from the powers of government that alone could authorize a compromise. It was necessary to break this circle; and my father went over the names of the men in Washington who might help us.

I could marvel at his understanding of these men and their motives, but we came to no plan of action until I spoke of what had been with me a sort of forlorn hope that I might appeal to President Cleveland himself.

My father said thoughfully: "What influence could you, a Republican, have with him? It's true that your youth may make an appeal—and the fact that you're pleading for your relatives, while not yourself a polygamist. But he would immediately ask us to abandon plural marriage, and that is established by a revelation from God which we cannot disregard. Even if the Prophet directed us, as a revelation from God, to abandon polygamy, still the nation would have further cause for quarrel because of the Church's temporal rule. No. I can make no promise. I can authorize no pledge. It must be for the Prophet of God to say what is the will of the Lord. You must see President Woodruff, and after he has asked for the will of the Lord I shall be content with his instruction."

Now, I do not wish to say—though I did then believe it—that the First Councillor of the Mormon Church was prepared to have the doctrine of plural marriage abandoned in order to have the people saved. It is impossible to predicate the thoughts of a man so diplomatic, so astute, and at the same time so deeply religious and so credulous of all the miracles of faith. He *did* believe in Divine guidance. He *was* sincere in his submission to the "revelations" of the Prophet. But, in the complexity of the mind of man, even such a faith may be complicated with the strategies of foresight, and the priest who bows devoutly to the oracle may yet, even unconsciously, direct the oracle to the utterance of his desire. And if my father was—as I suspected—considering a recession from plural marriage, he had as justification the basic "revelation," given through "Joseph the Prophet," commanding that the people should hold themselves in subjection to the government under which they lived, "until He shall come Whose right it is to rule."

We talked till midnight, in the quiet glow of the farmer's lamp-light, discussing possibilities, considering policies, weighing men; and then we parted—he to betake himself to whatever secure place of hiding he had found, and I to return to Ogden where I was then editing a newspaper. I was only twenty-nine years old, and the responsibility of the undertaking that had been entrusted to me weighed on my mind. I waited for a summons to confer with President Woodruff, but none came. Instead, my brother brought me word from the President that I must be "guided by the spirit of the Lord;" and, finally, my father sent me orders to consult the Second Councillor, Joseph F. Smith.

Joseph F. Smith! Since the death of the founder of the Mormon Church, there have been three men pre-eminent in its history: Brigham Young, who led the people across the desert into the Salt Lake Valley and established them in prosperity there; George Q. Cannon, who directed their policies and secured their national rights; and Joseph F. Smith, who today rules over that prosperity and markets that political right, like a Sultan. Of all these, Smith is, to the nation now, of most importance—and sinisterly so.

No Mormon in those years, I think, had more hate than Smith for the United States government; and surely none had better reasons to give himself for hate. He had the bitter recollection of the assassination of his father and his uncle in the jail of Carthage, Illinois; he could remember the journey that he had made with his widowed mother across the Mississippi, across Iowa, across the Missouri, and across the unknown and desert West, in ox teams, half starved, unarmed, persecuted by civilization and at the mercy of savages; he could remember all the toils and hardships of pioneer days "in the Valley;" he had seen the army of '58 arrive to complete, as he believed, the final destruction of our people; he had suffered from all the proscriptive legislation of "the raid," been outlawed, been in exile, been in hiding, hunted like a thief. He had been taught, and he

38

firmly believed, that the Smiths had been divinely appointed to rule, in the name of God, over all mankind. He believed that he—ordained a ruler over this world before ever the world was—had been persecuted by the hate and wickedness of men. He believed it literally; he preached it literally; he still believes and still preaches it. I did not then sympathize with this point of view, any more than I do now; but I did sympathize with him in the hardships that he had already endured and in the trials that he was still enduring—in common with the rest of us. The bond of community persecution intensified my loyalty. I felt for him almost as I felt for my own father. I went to him with the young man's trust in age made wise by suffering.

I had been directed to call on him in the President's offices, in Salt Lake City, where he was concealed, for the moment, under the name of "Mack"—the name that he used "on the underground"—and I went with my brother, late at night, to see him there. The President's offices were at that time in a little one-story plastered house that had been built by Brigham Young between two of his famous residences, the "Beehive House" and the "Lion House" (in which some twelve or fourteen of his wives had lived). The three houses were within the enclosure of a high cobblestone wall built by Brigham Young; and at night the great gate of the wall was shut and locked. We hammered discreetly on its panels of mountain pine, until a guard answered our knocking, recognized our voices and admitted us.

"He's in there," he said, pointing to the darkened windows of the offices—toward which he led us.

He unlocked the front door—having evidently locked it when he went to the gate—and he explained to a waiting attendant: "These brethren have an appointment. They wish to see Brother Mack."

The attendant led us down a dimly-lighted hall, through the public offices of the President into a rear room, a sort of retiring room, carpeted, furnished with bookcases, chairs, a table. The window blinds had all been carefully drawn.

Joseph F. Smith was waiting for us—a tall, lean, long-bearded man of a commanding figure—standing as if our arrival had stopped him in some anxious pacing of the carpet. His overcoat and his hat had been thrown on a chair. He greeted us with the air of one who is hurried, and sat down tentatively; and as soon as we came to the question of my trip to Washington, he broke out:

"These scoundrels here must be removed— if there's any way to do it. They're trying to repeat the persecutions of Missouri and Illinois. They want to despoil us of our heritage—of our families. I'm sick of being hunted like a wild beast. I've done no harm to them or theirs. Why can't they leave us alone to live our religion and obey the commandments of God and build up Zion?" He had begun to stride up and down the floor again, in a sort of driven and angry helplessness. "I thought Cleveland would stop this damnable raid and make them leave us in peace—but he's as bad as the rest. Can't they see that these carpet baggers are only trying to rob us? Make them see *that*. The hounds! Sometimes it seems to me that the Lord is letting these iniquities go on so that the nation may perish in its sins all the sooner!"

He sneered at John W. Young who had gone to Washington for the Church. (I had met Smith himself there, earlier in the year.) "I thought he'd accomplish something," he said, "with his fashionable home and his— He's using money enough! He's down there, taking things easy, while the rest of us are driven from pillar to post." He attacked the Federal authorities, Governor West, the "whole gang." He cried: "I love my wives and my children—whom the Lord gave me. I love them more than my life—more than anything in the world—except my religion! And here I am, fleeing from place to place, from the wrath of the wicked—and they're left in sorrow and suffering."

His face was pallid with emotion, and his voice came now hard with exasperation against his enemies and now husky with a passionate affection for his family—a man of fifty, gray-bearded, quivering in a nervous transport of excitement that jerked him up and down the room, gesticulating.

When he had worn out his first anger of revolt, I brought the conversation round to the question of polygamy, by asking him about a provisional constitution for statehood which the non-polygamous Mormons had recently adopted. It contained a clause making polygamy a misdemeanor. "I would have seen them all damned," he said, "before I would have yielded it, but I'm willing to try the experiment, if any good can come."

He had, I gathered, no aversion to "deceiving the wicked," but he was opposed to leading his people away from their loyalty to the doctrine of plural marriage, by conceding anything that might weaken their faith in it. And yet this impression may misrepresent him. He was too agitated, too exasperated, for any serious reflection on the situation.

My brother had gone—to keep some other engagement—and I stayed late, talking as long as Smith seemed to wish to talk. He rose at last and "blessed" me, his hands on my head, in a return to some larger trust in his religious authority; and I left him—with very doubtful and mixed emotions. His

42

natural violence and his lack of discipline
had been matters of common gossip among
our people, and I had heard of them from
childhood; but I had supposed that tribulations would, by this time, have matured him.
There was something compelling in his un-
softened turbulence, but nothing encouraging
for me as a messenger of conciliation. I felt
that there would be no help come from him
in my task, and I dropped him from my
reckoning.

I had made up my mind to a plan that was
almost as desperate as the conditions it sought
to cure—a plan that was in some ways so
absurd that I felt like keeping it concealed
for fear of ridicule—and I went about my
preparations for departure in a sort of hopeless hope. As the train drew out from Ogden,
I looked back at the mountains from my car
window, and saw again, in the spectacle of
their power, the pathos of our people—as if it
were the nation of my worship that bulked
there so huge above the people of my love—
and I, puny in my little efforts, going out to
plot an intercession, to appeal for a truce!
It was almost as if I were the son of a Con-
federate leader journeying to Washington,
on the eve of the Civil War, to attempt to
stand between North and South and hold
back their opposing armies, single-handed.

These are the things a man does when he
is young.

CHAPTER II

ON A MISSION TO WASHINGTON

I went discredited, as an envoy, by an incident of personal conflict with the Federal authorities; and I wish to relate that incident before I proceed any farther. I *must* relate it soon, because it came up for explanation in one of my first interviews with President Cleveland; and I wish to relate it now, because it was so typical of the day and the condition from which we had to save ourselves.

In the winter of 1885–6, the United States Marshals had been pursuing my father from place to place with such determined persistence that it was evident his capture was only a matter of time. We believed that if he were arrested and tried before Chief Justice Zane—with District Attorney Dickson and Assistant District Attorney Varian prosecuting—he would be convicted on so many counts that he would be held in prison indefinitely—that he might, in fact, end his days there. There was the rumor of a boast, to this effect, made by Federal officers; and we misunderstood them and their motives, in those days, sufficiently to accept the unjust report as well-founded.

My father, as First Councillor of the Church, had proposed to President Taylor that every man who was living in plural marriage should surrender himself voluntarily to the court and plead: "I entered into this covenant of celestial marriage with a personal conviction that it was an order revealed by our Father in Heaven for the salvation of mankind. I have kept my covenant in purity. I believed that no constitutional law of the country could forbid this practice of a religious faith. As the laws of Congress conflict with my sense of submission to the will of the Lord, I now offer myself, here, for whatever judgment the courts of my country may impose." He believed that such a course would vindicate the sincerity of the men who had engaged in polygamy and defied the law in an assumption of religious immunity; and he believed that the world would pause to reconsider its judgment upon us, if it saw thousands of men— the bankers, the farmers, the merchants, and all the religious leaders of a civilized community—marching in a mass to perform such an act of faith.

But President Taylor was not prepared for a movement that would have recommended itself better to the daring genius of Brigham Young. Taylor had given himself into the custody of the officers of the law once—in Carthage, Illinois—with Joseph Smith and his brother, Hyrum Smith; and Taylor had been wounded by the mob that broke into the jail and shot the Smiths to death. This, perhaps, had cured him of any faith in the protecting power of innocency. He decided against voluntary surrender; and now that my father's liberty was so seriously threatened, he ordered him to go either to Mexico or to the Sandwich Islands—his old mission field—where he would be beyond the reach of the United States authorities.

My father believed that if he left Utah, his recession might tend to placate the government and soften the severity of the prosecutions of the Mormons; and accordingly, on the night of February 12, 1886, he boarded a west-bound Central Pacific train at Willard. The Federal officers in some way learned of it; he was arrested, on the train, at Humboldt Wells, Nevada, and brought back to Utah. Near Promontory he fell from the steps of the moving car, at night, in the midst of an alkali desert, and hurt himself seriously. He was recaptured and brought to Salt Lake City on a stretcher, in a special car, guarded by a squad of soldiers from Fort Douglas, with loaded muskets, and a captain with a conspicuous sword. He was taken to Judge Zane's chambers and placed under bonds of $25,000. Immediately two bench warrants were issued by a United States Commissioner, and these were served upon him while he lay on a mattress on the floor of Zane's office. Two more

46

bonds of $10,000 each were given. He was then taken to his home.

Later—(President Taylor still insisting that he must not stand trial)—he disappeared again, "on the underground," and his bonds were declared forfeited. But in the meantime, while the grand jury was hearing testimony against him, one of the beloved women of his family was called for examination, and District Attorney Dickson asked her some questions that deeply wounded her. She returned home weeping. My brothers and I felt that the questions had been needlessly offensive, and after an indignant discussion of the matter, I undertook to remonstrate personally with Mr. Dickson.

If I had been as wise, then, as I sometimes *think* I am now, I should have realized that a meeting between us was dangerous; that the feeling, on our side at least, was too warm for calm remonstrances. And I should not have taken with me a younger brother, about sixteen years old, with all the hot-headedness of youth. Fortunately we did not go armed.

We sought Dickson in the evening, at the Continental Hotel—the old, adobe Continental with its wide porches and its lawn trees—and we found him in the lobby. I asked him to step out on the porch, where I might speak with him in private. He came without a moment's hesitation. He was a

47

big, handsome, black-bearded man in the prime of his strength.

We had scarcely exchanged more than a few sentences formally, when my brother drew back and struck him a smashing blow in the face. Dickson grappled with me, a little blinded, and I called to the boy to run— which he very wisely did. Dickson and I were at once surrounded, and I was arrested.

Ordinarily the incident would have been trivial enough, but in the alarmed state of the public mind it was magnified into an attempt on the part of George Q. Cannon's sons to take the life of the United States District Attorney. Indictments were found against my brother and myself, and against a cousin who happened to be in another part of the hotel at the time of the attack. Some weeks later, when the excitement had rather died down, I went to the District Attorney's office and arranged with his assistant, Mr. Varian, that the indictments against my brother (who had escaped from Utah) and my cousin (who was wholly innocent) should be quashed, and that I should plead guilty to a charge of assault and battery. On this understanding, I appeared in court before Chief Justice Zane.

But Mr. Varian, having consulted with Mr. Dickson, had learned that I had not struck the blow—though, as the elder brother, I was morally responsible for it—and he suggested to the court that sentence be suspended. This, Justice Zane seemed prepared to do, but I objected. I was a newspaper writer (as I explained), and I felt that if I criticized the court thereafter for what I believed to be a harshness that amounted to persecution, I could be silenced by the imposition of the suspended sentence; and if I failed to criticize, I should be false to what I considered my duty. I did not wish to be put in any such position; and I said so.

Justice Zane had a respect for the constitution and the statutes that amounted to a creed of infallibility. He was the most superbly rigid pontiff of legal justice that I ever knew. A man of unspotted character, a Puritan, of a sincerity that was afterwards accepted and admired from end to end of Utah, he was determined to vindicate the essential supremacy of the civil law over the ecclesiastical domination in the territory; and every act of insubordination against that law was resented and punished by him, unforgivingly. He promptly sentenced me to three months in the County Jail and a fine of $150.

My imprisonment was, of course, a farce. I was merely confined, most of the time, in a room in the County Court House, where I lived and worked as if I were in my home. But the sentence remained on my record as a sufficient mark of my recalcitrance; and I knew that it would not aid me in my appeal

to Washington, where I intended to argue—
as the first wise concession needed of the
Federal authorities—that Chief Justice Zane
should no longer be retained on the bench
in Utah, but should be succeeded by a man
more gentle. He was the great figure among
our prosecutors; the others were District
Attorney Dickson and the two assistants,
Mr. Varian and Mr. Hiles. The square had
only *seemed* to be broken by the recent retirement of Mr. Dickson; the strength of his
purpose remained still in power, in the person
of Judge Zane.

And let me say that whatever my opinion
was of these men, at that time, I recognize
now that they were justified as officers of
the law in enforcing the law. If it had not
been for them, the Mormon Church would
never have been brought to the point of
abating one jot of its pretensions. All four
men, as their records have since proved, were
much superior to their positions as territorial
officers. Utah's admiration for Judge Zane
was shown, upon the composition of our
differences with the nation, by the Mormon
vote that placed him on the Supreme Court
bench. Indeed, it is one of the strange
psychologies of this reconciliation, that, as
soon as peace was made, the strongest men
of both parties came into the warmest friendship; our fear and hatred of our prosecutors
changed to respect; and their opposition to

our indissoluble solidarity changed to regard
when they saw us devoting our strength to
purposes of which they could approve. But
now, in the midst of our contentions, the
aspect of splendor in their legal authority
had something baleful in it, for us; and we
saw our own defiance set with a halo of
martyrdom and illumined by the radiance
of a Church oppressed!

There was more than a glimmer of that
radiance in my thoughts as I made the railroad journey from Utah to the East. The
Union Pacific Railway, on which I rode,
followed the route that the Mormons had
taken in their long trek from the Missouri;
and I could look from my car window and
imagine them toiling across those endless
plains—in their creaking wagons, drawn by
their oxen and lean farm cows—choked with
dust, burned by the sun of the prairies, their
faces to the unknown dangers of an unknown
wilderness, and behind them the cool-roomed
houses, the moist fields, the tree-shaded
streets, all the quiet and comfort of the settled
life of homekeeping happiness that they had
left. My own mother had come that road,
a little girl of eight; and my mind was full
of pictures of her, at school in a wagon-box,
singing hymns with her elders around the
camp fires at night, or kneeling with the
mourners beside the grave of an infant relative
buried by the roadside. Our train crossed

the Loup Fork of the Platte almost within sight of the place where my father, a lad of twenty, had led across the river at nightfall, had been lost to his party, and had nearly perished, naked to the cold, before he struggled back to the camp. I could see their little circle of wagons drawn up at sunset against the menace of the Indians who snaked through the long grass to kill. I could feel some of their despair, and my heart lifted to their heroism. Never had such a migration been made by any people with fewer of the concomitants of their civilization. Their arms had been taken from them at Nauvoo; they had bartered their goods for wagons and cattle to carry them; even the grain that they brought, for food, had to be saved for seed. They felt themselves devoted to destruction by the people with whose laws and institutions they had come in conflict, and they went forth bravely, trusting in the power of the God whom they were determined to worship according to their despised belief.

Now they had built themselves new homes and meeting-houses in the fertile "Valley;" and the civilization that they had left, having covered the distance of their exile, was punishing them again for their law-breaking fidelity to their faith. Surely they had suffered enough! Surely it was evident that suffering only made them strong to resist!

52

Surely there must be somebody in power in Washington who could be persuaded to see that, where force had always failed, there might be some profit in employing gentleness!

This, at least, was the appeal which I had planned to make. And I had decided to make it through Mr. Abraham S. Hewitt, then mayor of New York City, who had been a friend of my father in Congress. He was not in favor with the administration at Washington. He was personally unfriendly to President Cleveland. I was a stranger to him. But I had seen enough of him to know that he had the heart to hear a plea on behalf of the Mormons, and the brain to help me carry that plea diplomatically to President Cleveland.

When I arrived in New York I set about finding him without the aid of any common friend. I did not try to reach him at his home, being aware that he might resent an intrusion of public matters upon his private leisure, and fearing to impair my own confidence by beginning with a rebuff. I decided to see him in his office hours.

I cannot recall why I did not find him in the municipal buildings, but I well remember going to and fro in the streets in search of him, feeling at every step the huge city's absorption in its own press and hurry of affairs, and seeing the troubles of Utah as distant as a foreign war. It was with a very keen sense of discouragement that I took my place, at last, in the long line of applicants waiting for a word with the man who directed the municipal activities of this tremendous hive of eager energy.

He was in the old Stewart building, on Broadway, near Park Place; and he had his desk in what was, I think, a temporary office—an empty shop used as an office—on the ground floor. There must have been fifty men ahead of me, and they were the unemployed, as I remember it, besieging him for work. They came to his desk, spoke, and passed with a rapidity that was ominous. As I drew nearer, I watched him anxiously, and saw the incessant, nervous, querulous activity of eyes, lips, hands, as he dismissed each with a word or a scratch of the pen, and looked up sharply at the next one.

"Well, young man," he greeted me, "what do *you* want?"

I replied: "I want a half hour of your time."

"Good God," he said, in a sort of reproachful indignation, "I couldn't give it to the President of the United States."

I felt the crowd of applicants pressing behind me. I knew the man's prodigious humanity. I knew that if I could only hold them back long enough—"Mr. Hewitt," I said, "it's more important even than *that*. It's to save a whole people from suffering—from destruction."

He may have thought me a maniac; or it may be that the desperation of the moment sounded in my voice. He frowned intently up at me. "Who *are* you?"

"I'm the son of your old friend in Congress, George Q. Cannon of Utah," I said. "My father's in exile. He and his people are threatened with endless proscriptions. I want time to tell you."

His impatience had vanished. His eyes were steadily kind and interested. "Can you come to the Board of Health, in an hour? As soon as I open the meeting, I'll retire and listen to you."

I asked him for a card, to admit me to the meeting, having been stopped that morning at many doors. He gave it, nodded, and flashed his attention on the man behind me. I went out with the heady assurance that my first move had succeeded; but I went, too, with the restrained pulse of realizing that I had yet to join issue with the decisive event and do it warily.

I do not remember where I found the Board of Health in session. I recall only the dark, official board-room, the members at the table, and—as the one small spot of light and interest to me—Mr. Hewitt's white-bearded face, as an attendant opened the door to me, and the Mayor, looking up alertly, nodded across the room, and waved his hand to a chair.

As soon as he had opened the meeting, we

withdrew together to a settee in some remote corner, and I began to tell him, as quickly as I could, the desperateness of the Mormon situation. "Yes," he said, "but why can't your people obey the law?"

I explained what I have been trying to explain in this narrative—that these people, following a Church which they believed to be guided by God, and regarding themselves as objects of a religious persecution, could not be brought by means of force to obey a law against conscience. I explained that I was not pleading to save their pride but to spare them useless suffering; their history showed that no proscription, short of extermination outright, could overcome their resistance; but what force could not accomplish, a little sensible diplomacy might hope to effect. No first step could be made, by them, towards a composition of their differences with the law so long as the law was administered with a hostility that provoked hostility. But if we could obtain some mitigation of the law's severity, the leaders of the Church were willing to surrender themselves to the court—such of them as had not already died of their privations or served their terms of imprisonment— and a sense of gratitude for leniency would prepare the way for a recession from their present attitude of unconquerable antagonism.

He listened gravely, knowing the situation from his own experience in Congress, and checking off the items of my argument with a nod of acceptance that came, often, before I had completed what I had to say. He asked: "Do you know President Cleveland?"

I told him that I had seen the President several times but was not known to him.

"Well," he said, "I may be able to help you indirectly. I don't care for Cleveland, and I wouldn't ask him for a favor if I were sinking. But tell me what plan you have in your mind, and I'll see if I can't aid you—through friends."

I replied that I hoped to have some man appointed as Chief Justice in Utah who should adopt a less rigorous way of adjudicating upon the cases of polygamists; but that before he was selected—or at least before he knew of his appointment—I wished to talk with him and convert him to the idea that he could begin the solution of "the Mormon question" by having the leaders of the community come into his court and accept sentences that should not be inconsistent with the sovereignty of the law but not unmerciful to the subjects of that sovereignty.

"The man you want," Mr. Hewitt said, "is here in New York—Elliot F. Sandford. He's a referee of the Supreme Court of this state—a fine man, great legal ability, courageous, of undoubted integrity. Come to me, tomorrow. I'll introduce you to him."

It was the first time that I had even heard

the name of Elliot F. Sandford; and I had not
the faintest notion of how best to approach him.

I did not find him in Mr. Hewitt's office,
on the morrow; but the Mayor had communicated with him, and now gave me a
letter of introduction to him; and I went
alone to present it.

He received me in his outer office, with a
manner full of kindliness but non-committal.
He glanced through my letter of introduction,
and I tried to read him while he did it. He
was not on the surface. He was a tall, dig-
nified man, his hair turning gray—thoughtful,
judicial—evidently a man who was not quick
to decide. He led me into his private room,
and sat down with the air of a lawyer who has
been asked to take a case and who wishes
first to hear all the details of the action.

I began by describing the Mormon situation
as I saw it in those days: that the Mormons
were growing more desperately determined
in their opposition, because they believed
their prosecutors were persecuting them;
that the District Attorney and his assistants
were harsh to the point of heartlessness, and
that Judge Zane (to us, then) acted like a
religious fanatic in his judicial office; that
nearly every Federal official in Utah had taken
a tone of bigoted opposition to the people;
and that the law was detested and the government despised because of the actions of
Federal "carpet-baggers."

I was prejudiced, no doubt, and partisan in my account of the state of affairs, but I did not exaggerate the facts as I saw them; I believed what I said.

I did not really reach his sympathy until I spoke of the court system in Utah—the open venire, the employment of "professional jurors"—the legal doctrine of "segregation," under which a man might be separately indicted for every day of his living in plural marriage—and the result of all this: that the pursuit of defendants and the confiscation of property had become less an enforcement of law than a profitable legal industry.

After two hours of argument and examination, I ended with an appeal to him to accept the opportunity to undertake a merciful assuagement of our misery. After so many years of failure on the part of the Federal authorities, he might have the distinction of calling into his court the Mormon leaders who had been most long and vainly sought by the law; and by sentencing them to a supportable punishment, he could begin the composition of a conflict that had gone on for half a century.

He replied with reasons that expressed a kindly unwillingness to undertake the work. It would mean the sacrifice of his professional career in New York. He would be putting himself entirely outside the progression of advancement. His friends, here, would never understand why he had done it. The affairs of Utah had little interest for them.

I saw that he was not convinced. His wife had been waiting some minutes in the outer office; he proposed that he should bring her in; and I gathered from his manner, that he expected her to pronounce against his accepting my solicitation, and so terminate our interview pleasantly, with the aid of the feminine social grace.

Mrs. Sandford, when she entered, certainly looked the very lady to do the thing with gentle skill. She was handsome, with an animated expression, dark-eyed, dark-haired, charming in her costume, a woman of the smiling world, but maturely sincere and unaffected. I took a somewhat distracted impression of her greeting, and heard him begin to explain my proposal to her, as one hears a "silent partner" formally consulted by a man who has already made up his mind. But when I glanced at her, seated, her manner had changed. She was listening as if she were used to being consulted and knew the responsibilities of decision. She had the abstracted eye of impersonal consideration— silent—with now and then a slow, meditative glance at me.

Her first question seemed merely femininely curious as to the domestic aspects of polygamy. How did the women endure it?

I repeated a conversation I had once had

with Frances Willard, who had said: "The woman's heart must ache in polygamy." To which I had made the obvious reply: "Don't women's hearts ache all over the world? Is there any condition of society in which women do not bear more than an equal share of the suffering?"

Mrs. Sandford asked me pointedly whether I was living in polygamy?

No, I was not.

Did I believe in it?

I believed that those *did* who practised it.

Why didn't I practise it?

Those who practised it believed that it had been authorized by a divine revelation. I had not received such a revelation. I did not expect to.

Our talk warmed into a very intimate discussion of the lives of the Mormon people, but I supposed that she was moved only by a curiosity to which I was accustomed—a curiosity that was not necessarily sympathetic —the curiosity one might have about the domestic life of a Mohammedan. I took advantage of her curiosity to lead up to an explanation of how the proscription of polygamy was driving young Mormons into the practice, instead of frightening them from it. And so I arrived at another recountal of the miserable condition of persecution and suffering which I had come to ask her husband help us relieve; and I made my appeal again, to them both, with something of despair, because of my failure with him, and perhaps with greater effect because of my despair. She listened thoughtfully, her hands clasped.

It did not seem that I had reached her—until she turned to him, and said unexpectedly "It seems to me that this is an opportunity—a larger opportunity than any I see *here*—to do a great deal of good."

He did not appear as surprised as I was. He made some joking reference to his income and asked her if she would be willing to live on a salary of—How much was the salary of the Chief Justice of Utah?

I thought it was about $3,000 a year.

"Two hundred and fifty dollars a month," he said. "How many bonnets will that buy?"

"No," she retorted, "you can't put the blame on my millinery bill. If *that's* been the cause of your hesitation, I'll agree to dress as becomes the wife of a poor but upright judge."

In such a happy spirit of good-natured raillery, my petition was provisionally entertained, till I could see the President; and it is one of the curiosities of experience, as I look back upon it now, that a decision so momentous in the history of Utah owed its induction to the wisdom of a woman and was confirmed with a domestic pleasantry.

I left them after we had arrived at the tacit understanding that if President Cleveland

should make the appointment, Mr. Sandford
would accept it with the end in view that I had
proposed. I went to report my progress, in
a cipher telegram, to Salt Lake City, and I
recall the peculiarly mixed satisfaction with
which I regarded my work, as I walked the
streets of New York after this interview. In
all that city of millions, I knew, there were
few if any men who were the equal of my
father in the essentials of manhood; and yet,
before he could enjoy the liberties of which
they were so lightly unconscious, he must
endure the shame of a prison. I was rejoicing
because I was succeeding in getting for him a
sentence that should not be ruinous! I was
pleased because a prospective judge had been
persuaded to be not too harsh to him!

It did not make me bitter. I realized that
the peculiar faith which we had accepted was
responsible for our peculiar suffering. I saw
that we were working out our human destiny;
and if that destiny was not of God, but merely
the issue of human impulsion, still our only
prospect of success would come of our bearing
with experience patiently to make us strong.

When I went back to Mr. Hewitt, to tell
him of my success, I consulted with him upon
the best way of approaching Mr. Cleveland.
And he was not encouraging. In his opinion
of the President, he had, as I could see, the
impatient resentment which a quick-minded,
nervous, small-bodied man has for the big,

slow one whose mental operations are stubbornly deliberate and leisurely. And he was obviously irritated by the President's continual assumption that he was better than his party. "He's honest," he said, "by right of original discovery of what honesty is. No one can question his honesty. But as soon as he discovers a better thing than he knew previously, he announces it as if it were the discovery of a new planet. It may have been a commonplace for a generation. That doesn't signify. He announces it with such ponderosity that the world believes it's as prodigious as his sentences!"

As for my own mission: I would have to be persistent, patient, and—lucky. "You'll have to be lucky, if you intend to persuade him to acquire any information. He's been so successful in instructing mankind that it's hard to get him to see he doesn't know all he ought to know about a public question. But he's honest and he's courageous. If you can convince him that your view is right, he'll carry out the conviction in spite of everything. In fact he'll be all the better pleased if it requires fearlessness and defiance of general sentimentality *to* carry it out."

He gave me a letter to Mr. William C. Whitney, then Secretary of the Navy, explaining my purpose in coming to Washington, and asking him to obtain for me an interview with President Cleveland without using Mr.

Hewitt's name. Then he shook hands with me, and wished me success. "I have the faith," he said, "that is without hope."

That expressed my own feeling. The faith that was without hope!

CHAPTER III

WITHOUT A COUNTRY

So I came to Washington. So I entered the capital of the government that commanded my allegiance and inspired my fear. I wonder whether another American ever saw that city with such eyes of envy, of aspiration, of wistful pride, of daunted admiration. Here were all the consecrations of a nation's memories, and they thrilled me, even while they pierced me with the sense that I was not, and might well despair of ever being, a citizen of their glory. Here were the monuments of patriotism in Statuary Hall, erected to the men whose histories had been the inspiration of my boyhood; and I remember how I stood before them, conscious that I was now almost an outlaw from their communion of splendor. I remember how I saw, with an indescribable conflict of feelings, the ranked graves of the soldiers in the cemetery at Arlington, and recollected that this very ground had been taken from General Lee, that heroic opponent of Federal authority—and read the tablet, "How sleep the brave who sink to rest by all their country's wishes bless'd,"—and bowed in spirit to the nation's benediction upon the men who had upheld its power. I was awed

66

by a prodigious sense of the majesty of that power. I saw with fear its immovability to the struggles of our handful of people. And at night, walking under the trees of Lafayette Park, with all the odors of the southern Spring among the leaves, I looked at the lighted front of the White House and realized that behind the curtains of those quiet windows sat the ruler who held the almost absolute right of life and death over our community—as if it were the palace of a Czar that I must soon enter, with a petition for clemency, which he might refuse to entertain!

When I had been in Washington, four years before, as secretary to Delegate John T. Caine of Utah, I had felt a younger assurance that our resistance would slowly wear out the Federal authority and carry us through to statehood. Four years of disaster had starved out that hope. The proposition had been established that Congress had supreme control over the territories; and there was no virtue either in our religious assumption of warrant to speak for God, or in our plea of inherent constitutional right to manage our own affairs. Thirty years earlier, my father had been elected Senator from the proposed state of Utah, and he had been rejected. In thirty years so little progress had been made! The way that was yet to travel seemed very long and very dark.

Out of this mood of despondence I had to lift myself by an act of will. There, Washington itself helped me against itself. I made a pilgrimage of courage to its commemorations of courage, and drew an inspiration of hope from its monuments to the achievements of its past. And particularly I went to the house in which my father had lived when he had had his part in the statesman life of the capital, and animated my resolution with the thought that I *must* succeed in order that he might be restored in public honor.

I narrate all this personal incident of emotion in the hope that it may help to explain a success that might otherwise seem inexplicable. The Mormon Church had, for years, employed every art of intrigue and diplomacy to protect itself in Washington. I wish to make plain that it was not by any superior cunning of negotiation that my mission succeeded. I undertook the task almost without instruction; I performed it without falsehood; I had nothing in my mind but an honest loyalty for my own people, a desire to be a citizen of my native country, and a filial devotion to the one man in the world whom I most admired.

When I delivered my letter of introduction from Mr. Hewitt to Mr. William C. Whitney, Secretary of the Navy, I found him very busy with his work in his department—carrying out the plans that established the modern

American navy and entitled him to be called the "father" of it. He withdrew from the men who were discussing designs and figures at a table in his room, and sat with me before a window that looked out upon the White House and its grounds; and he listened to me, interestedly, genially, but with a thought still (as I could see) for the affairs that my arrival had interrupted. He struck me as a man who was used to having many weighty matters together on his mind, without finding his attention crowded by them all, and without being impatient in his consideration of any.

I developed with him an idea which I had been considering: that the President might not only help the Mormons by taking up their case, but might gain political prestige for the coming campaign for re-election, by adjusting the dissentions in Utah. He heard me with a twinkle. He thought an interview might be arranged. He made an appointment to see me in the afternoon and to have with him Colonel Daniel S. Lamont, the President's secretary, who was then Mr. Cleveland's political "trainer."

My meeting with Colonel Lamont, in the afternoon, began jocularly. "This," Mr. Whitney introduced me, "is the young man who has a plan to use that mooted—and booted—Mormon question to re-elect the President."

"Hardly that, Mr. Secretary," I said. "I have a plan to help my father and his colleagues to regain their citizenship. If President Cleveland's re-election is essential to it, I suppose I must submit. You know I'm a Republican."

They laughed. We sat down. And I found at once that Colonel Lamont understood the situation in Utah, thoroughly. He had often discussed it, he said, with the Church's agents in Washington. I went over the situation with him, as I had gone over it with Mr. Sandford, in careful detail. He seemed surprised at my assurance that my father and the other proscribed leaders of the Church would submit themselves to the courts if they could do so on the conditions that I proposed; I convinced him of the possibility by referring him to Mr. Richards, the Church's attorney in Washington, for a confirmation of it. I pointed out that if these leaders surrendered, President Cleveland could be made the direct beneficiary, politically, of their composition with the law.

Colonel Lamont was a small, alert man with a conciseness of speech and manner that is associated in my memory with the bristle of his red moustache cut short and hard across a decisive mouth. He radiated nervous vitality; and I understood, as I studied him, how President Cleveland, with his infinite patience for detail, had survived so well in the multitudinous duties of his office—having as his secretary a man born with the ability to cut away the non-essentials, and to pass on to Mr. Cleveland only the affairs worthy of his careful deliberation.

I was doubtful whether I should tell Colonel Lamont and Mr. Whitney of my conversation with Mr. Sandford. I decided that their considerateness entitled them to my full confidence, and I told them all—begging them, if I was indiscreet or undiplomatic, to charge the offence to my lack of experience rather than to debit it against my cause.

They passed it off with banter. It was understood that the President should not be told—and that I should not tell him—of my talk with Mr. Sandford. Colonel Lamont undertook to arrange an audience with Mr. Cleveland for me. "You had better wait," he said, "until I can approach him with the suggestion that there's a young man here, from Utah, whom he ought to see."

I knew, then, that I was at least well started on the open road to success. I knew that if Colonel Lamont said he would help me, there would be no difficulties in my way except those that were large in the person of the President himself.

Two days later I received the expected word from Colonel Lamont, and I went to the White House as a man might go to face his own trial. I met the secretary in one of the eastern upstairs rooms of the official apartments; and after the usual crowd had passed out, he led me into the President's office—which then overlooked the Washington monument, the Potomac and the Virginia shore. Mr. Cleveland was working at his desk. Colonel Lamont introduced me by name, and added, "the young man from Utah, of whom I spoke."

The President did not look up. He was signing some papers, bending heavily over his work. It took him a moment or two to finish; then he dropped his pen, pushed aside the papers, turned awkwardly in his swivel chair and held out his hand to me. It was a cool, firm hand, and its grasp surprised me, as much as the expression of his eyes—the steady eyes of complete self-control, composure, intentness.

I had come with a prejudice against him; I was a partisan of Mr. Blaine, whom he had defeated for the Presidency; I believed Mr. Blaine to be the abler man. But there was something in Mr. Cleveland's hand and eyes to warn me that however slow-moving and even dull he might appear, the energy of a firm will compelled and controlled him. It stiffened me into instant attention.

He made some remark to Colonel Lamont to indicate that our conversation was to occupy about half an hour. He asked me to be seated in a chair at the right-hand side

72

of his desk. He said almost challengingly: "You're the young man they want I should talk to about the Utah question."

The tone was not exactly unkind, but it was not inviting. I said, "Yes, sir."

He looked at me, as a judge might eye the suspect of circumstantial evidence. "You're the son of one of the Mormon leaders."

I admitted it.

And then he began.

He began with an account of what he had done to compose the differences in Utah. He explained and justified the appointments he had made there—appointments that had been recommended by Southern senators and representatives who, because they were Southerners, were opposed to the undue extension and arbitrary use of Federal power. He had made Caleb W. West of Kentucky governor of Utah on the recommendation of Senator Blackburn of Kentucky, my father's friend. He had made Frank H. Dyer, originally of Mississippi, United States Marshal. He had appointed a District Attorney in whom he had every confidence. He had a right to believe that these men, recommended by the statesmen of the South, would execute and adjudicate the laws in Utah according to the most lenient Southern construction of Federal rights. He dwelt upon Governor West's charitable intentions towards the Mormon leaders, went over West's efforts at pacification in accurate detail, and told of West's chagrin at his failure—with an irritation that showed how disappointed he himself was with the continued recurrence of the Mormon troubles.

I had to tell him that the situation had not improved, and his face flushed with an anger that he made no attempt to conceal. He declared that the fault must lie in our obstinate determination to hold ourselves superior to the law. He could not sympathize with our sufferings, he said, since they were self-inflicted. He admitted that he had once been opposed to the Edmunds-Tucker bill, but felt now that it was justified by the immovability of the Mormons. All palliatives had failed. The patience of Congress had been exhausted. There was no recourse, except to make statutes cutting enough to destroy the illegal practices and unlawful leadership in the Mormon community.

"Mr. President," I pleaded, "I've lived in Utah all my life. I know these people from both points of view. You know of the situation only from Federal office holders who consider it solely with regard to their official responsibility to you and to the country. Why not learn what the Mormons think?"

He replied that it was not within the province of the President—his power or his duty— to consider the mental attitude of men who were opposing the enforcement of the law.

74

It was an inexcusable offence against the general welfare that one community should be rising continually against the Federal authority and occupying the time and attention of Congress with a determined recalcitrance.

For an hour, he continued, with vigor and dignity, to describe the situation as he saw it; and he chilled me to the heart with his determination to concede nothing more to a community that had refused to be placated by what he had already conceded. I listened without trying, without even wishing, to interrupt him; for I had been warned by Mr. Whitney and Colonel Lamont that it would be wise to let him deliver himself of his opinion before attempting to influence him to a milder one; and I could not contradict anything that he said, for he made no misstatements of fact.

Colonel Lamont had entered once, and had withdrawn again when he saw that Mr. Cleveland was still talking. At the end of about an hour, the President rose. "Mr. Cannon," he said, "I don't see what more I can do than has already been done. Tell your people to obey the law, as all other citizens are required to obey it, and they'll find that their fellow-citizens of this country will do full justice to their heroism and their other good qualities. If the law seems harsh, tell them that there's an easy way to avoid its cruelty by simply getting out from under its condemnation."

His manner indicated that the conference was at an end. He reached out his hand as if to drop the subject then and forever, as far as I was concerned. "Mr. President," I asked, with the composure of desperation, "do you really want to settle the Mormon question?"

He looked at me with the first gleam of humor that had shown in his eyes—and it was a humor of peculiar richness and unction. "Young man," he asked, "what have I been saying to you all this time? What have I been working for, ever since I first took up the consideration of this subject at the beginning of my term?"

"Mr. President," I replied, "if you were travelling in the West, and came to an unbridged stream with your wagon train, and saw tracks leading down into the water where you thought there was a ford, you would naturally expect to cross there, assuming that others had done so before you. But suppose that some man on the bank should say to you: 'I've watched wagon trains go in here for more than twenty years, and I've never yet seen one come out on the other side. Look over at that opposite bank. You see there are no wagon tracks *there*. Now, down the river a piece, is a place where I *think* there's a ford. I've never got anybody to try it yet, but certainly it's as good a chance as this one!' Mr. President, what would you do? Would you attempt a crossing where there had been twenty years of failure, or would you try the other place—on the chance that it might take you over?"

He had been regarding me with slowly fading amusement that gave way to an expression of grave attention.

"I've been watching this situation for several years," I went on, "and it seems to me that there's the possibility of a just, a humane, and a final settlement of it, by getting the Mormon leaders to come voluntarily into court—and it can be done!—with the assurance that the object of the administration is to correct the community evil—not to exterminate the Mormon Church or to persecute its 'prophets,' but to secure obedience to the law and respect for the law, and to lead Utah into a worthy statehood."

I paused. He thought a moment. Then he said: "I can't talk any longer, now. Make another appointment with Lamont. I want to hear what you have to say." And he dismissed me.

Colonel Lamont told me to come back on the following afternoon; and I went away with the dubious relief of feeling that if I had not yet won my case I had, at least, succeeded in having judgment reserved. I went to work to arrange my arguments for the morrow, to make them as concise as possible and to divide them into brief chapters in case I should have as little opportunity for extended explanations as the President had been giving me. I saw that the whole matter was gloomy and oppressive to him—that his responsibility was as dark on his mind as our sufferings—and I took the hint of his amused interest, in order to work out ways of brightening the subject with anecdote and illustration.

I saw Colonel Lamont on the morrow, and he beamed a congratulation on me. "You've aroused his curiosity," he said. "You've interested him."

He had made an appointment some days ahead; and when I entered the President's office to keep that appointment, I found Mr. Cleveland at his desk, as if he had not moved in the interval, laboriously reading and signing papers as before. It gave me an impression of immovability, of patient and methodical relentlessness that was disheartening.

But as soon as he turned to me, I found him another man. He was interested, receptive, almost genial. He gave me an opportunity to cover the whole ground of my case, and I went over it step by step. He showed no emotion when I recited some of the incidents of pathetic suffering among our people; and at first he seemed doubtful whether he should be amused by the humorous episodes that I narrated. But I did not wish merely to amuse him; I was trying to convey to his mind (without saying so) that so long as a people could suffer and laugh too, they could never be overcome by the mere reduplication of their sufferings. He looked squarely at me, with a most determined front, when I told him that the Mormons would be ground to powder before they would yield. "They *can't* yield," I warned him. "They're like the passengers on a train going with a mad speed down a dangerous grade. For any of them to attempt to jump is simple destruction. They can only pray to Providence to help them. But if that train were to be brought to a stop at some station where they could alight with anything like self-respect, there would be many of them glad to get off—even though the train had *not* arrived at its 'revealed' destination."

I do not remember—and if I did, it would be tedious to relate—the exact sequence and progression of argument in this interview and the *dozen* others that succeeded it. Mr. Cleveland became more and more interested in the Mormon people, their family life, their religion, and their politics. He was as painstaking in acquiring information about them as he was in performing all the other duties of his office. I might have been discouraged by the number and apparent ineffectiveness of my interviews with him, had not Colonel

Lamont kept me informed of the growth of the President's good feeling and of his genuinely paternal interest in the people of Utah. It became more than a personal desire with Mr. Cleveland to benefit politically by a settlement of the Mormon troubles, if indeed he had ever had such a desire. His humanity was enlisted, his conscience appealed to.

He asked me, once, if I knew anything of Mr. Sandford, and I replied that I knew him and believed in him. He told me, at last, that he was going to appoint Mr. Sandford Chief Justice of Utah, and added significantly, " I suppose he will get in touch with the situation." I accepted this remark as a permission to confer with Mr. Sandford, and I journeyed to New York to see him and to renew the understanding I had with him.

He was appointed Chief Justice on the 9th day of July, 1888, and—as the Mormon people expressed it—"the backbone of the raid was broken." On August 26, 1888, he arrived in Salt Lake City. On September 17, my father came before him in court and pleaded guilty to two indictments charging him with "unlawful cohabitation." He was fined $450 and sentenced to the penitentiary for one hundred and seventy-five days. His example was followed by a number of prominent Mormons, including Francis Marion Lyman, who is today the President of the Quorum of the twelve Apostles and next in rank for the Presidency. It is true that not many cases, relatively speaking, came to Justice Sandford; but the leader whom the authorities were most eager to subjugate under Federal power was judged and sentenced; and the effect, both on the country and on the Mormon people, was all that we had expected.

There are memories in a man's life that have a peculiar value. One such, to me, is the picture I have in mind of my father undergoing his penitentiary sentence, wearing his prison clothes with an unconsciousness that makes me still feel a pride in the power of the human soul to rise superior to the deformities of circumstance. Charles Wilcken (whom I have described driving us to Bountiful) was visiting him one day in the prison office, when a guard entered with his hat on. Wilcken snatched it from his head. "Never enter *his* presence," he said, "without taking it off." And the guard never did again. . . . I salute the memory. I come to it with my head bare and my back stiffened. I see in that calm face the possibilities of the human spirit. He was *a man!*

He spent his time, there, as he would have spent it elsewhere, writing, conferring with the agents of his authority, planning for his people. I saw he was aware that he would emerge from his imprisonment a free man, personally, but still enslaved by the conditions of the community; and I knew that he would use his freedom to free the others. I knew that he had accepted his sentence with this end in view. In plain words, I knew now— though he never said so—that he was looking toward the necessary recession from the doctrine of polygamy, and that he may have counted on the spectacle of his imprisonment to help prepare his people for a general submission to the law.

With the entry of these leaders into prison, the Mormons felt for them a warmer admiration, a deeper reverence; but it was mingled with a gratitude to the nation for the leniency of the court and an awed sense, too, of the power of the civil law. President Woodruff secretly and tentatively withdrew his necessary permission, as head of the Church, to the solemnization of any more plural marriages; and he ordered the demolition of the Endowment House in which such marriages had been chiefly celebrated. Many of the non-Mormons, who had despaired of any solution of the troubles in Utah, now began to hope. The country had been impoverished; the Mormons had been deprived of much of their substance and financial vigor; and reasons of business prudence among the Gentiles weighed against a continuance of proscription. Some of them distrusted the motives of their own leaders more than they did the Mormon people. Some were weary of the quarrel. For humane reasons, for business reasons, for the sake of young Utah, it was argued that the persecution should end.

But in the years 1888 and 1889, thousands of newcomers arrived in Utah with a strong antagonism to the religion and the political authority of the Mormon Church; and, with the growth of Gentile population, there came a natural determination on their part to obtain control of the local governments of cities and counties. In opposing this movement, the power of the Church was again solidified. By 1889, the Gentiles had taken the city governments of Ogden and Salt Lake City, had elected members of the legislature in Salt Lake County, and had carried the passage of a Public School Bill, against the timid and secret opposition of the Church. President Cleveland had been defeated and succeeded by President Harrison; and Chief Justice Sandford had been removed and Chief Justice Zane reinstated. (He did not adjudicate with his previous rigor, however,— because of the success of Justice Sandford's policy of leniency.) The Church made no move publicly to repudiate polygamy, and its silent attitude of defiance, in this regard, gave a battle cry to all its enemies.

The crisis was precipitated by a movement that had begun in the territory of Idaho, where the Mormons had been disfranchised by means of a test oath—(a provision still remaining in the Idaho state constitution, but now nullified by the political power of the Mormon leaders in Salt Lake City.) A bill, known as the Cullom-Struble bill, was introduced at Washington, to do in Utah what had been done in Idaho.

The Church was then directed by President Woodruff and his two Councillors, George Q. Cannon and Joseph F. Smith. But President Woodruff was as helpless in the political world as a nun. He was a gentle, earnest old man, patiently ingenuous and simple-minded, with a faith in the guidance of Heaven that was only greater than my father's because it was unmixed with any earthly sagacity. He had the mind, and the appearance, of a country preacher, and even when he was "on the underground" he used to do his daily "stint" of farm labor, secretly, either at night or in the very early morning. He was a successful farmer (born in Connecticut), of a Yankee shrewdness and industry. He recognized that in order to get a crop of wheat, it was necessary to do something more than trust in the Lord. But in administering the affairs of the Church, he seemed to have no such sophistication.

I can see him yet, at the meetings of the Presidency, opening his mild blue eyes in surprised horror at a report of some new danger threatening us. "My conscience! My conscience!" he would cry. "Is that so, brother!" When he was assured that it was so, he would say, resignedly: "The Lord will look after us!" And then, after a silence, turning to his First Councillor, he would ask: "What do you think we ought to do, Brother George Q. ?"

The Second Councillor, Joseph F. Smith, sat at these meetings, in a saturnine reserve and silence, either nursing his concealed thought or having none. When a decision had been suggested, he was appealed to and added his assent. It always seemed to me that he was sulkily sleepy; but this impression may have come from the contrast of the First Councillor's mental alertness and the bright cheerfulness of the President—who never, to my knowledge, showed the slightest bitterness against anybody. President Woodruff believed that all the persecutions of the Mormons were due to the Devil's envy of the Lord's power as it showed itself in the establishment of the Mormon Church: and he assumed that the Gentiles did the work they were tempted to do against us, because the Holy Spirit had not yet ousted the evil from their souls. He had no fear of the ultimate triumph of the Church, because he had no fear of the ultimate triumph of God. Whenever he could escape for a day from the worldly duties of his office, he went fishing!

When the progress of the Cullom-Struble bill began to make its threatening advance, my father went secretly to Washington; and a short time afterwards, word came to me in Ogden, through the Presidency, that he wished me to arrange my business affairs for a long absence from Utah, and follow him to the capital.

I found him there, in the office of Delegate John T. Caine of Utah—the cluttered office of a busy man—and he explained, composedly, why he had sent for me. The Cullom-Struble bill had been favorably considered by the Senate Committee on Territories, and the disfranchisement of all the Mormons of Utah seemed imminent. Every argument, political or legal, had been used against the measure, in vain. Since I, a non-polygamous Mormon, would be disfranchised if the bill became law, he thought I might be a good advocate against it. He said: "I have not appeared in the matter. None of our friends know that I am here. If it were known, it might only increase our difficulties. Say nothing of it. We have been at a disadvantage with a Republican administration because most of our prominent men are Democrats. You were so effective with the Democrats, let us see what you can do now with your own party friends."

After taking his advice, I went to see Senator Henry M. Teller, of Colorado, who was a friend of my father and of the Mormon people. He admitted that the situation was desperate. He proposed that I should speak before the committees of both houses; they might listen to *me* as a Republican who had no official rank in the Church and no political authority. He offered to introduce me to any of the Senators and members of Congress, but advised that I should rather go unintroduced, without influence, and make my appeal as a private citizen.

This sounded to me depressingly like the call to lead a "forlorn hope." I reported to my father again, and was not altogether reassured by a tranquility which he seemed to be able to maintain in the face of any desperation. Other agencies of the Church had reached the end of their resources. There was no help in sight. And I went, at last, to throw our case upon the mercy of the Secretary of State, Mr. James G. Blaine, my father's friend, the friend of our people, the statesman whom I—in common with millions of other Americans—regarded with a reverence that approached idolatry.

He received me in the long room of the Secretary's apartments, standing, a striking figure in black, against the rich and heavy background of the official furnishing. He was very pale—unhealthily so—perhaps with the progress of the disease of which he was to die in so short a time. In contrast with his usual brilliancy of mind, he seemed to me, at first, depressed and quiet—with a kindly serenity of manner, at once gracious, and intimate, but masterful.

He was instantly and deeply interested in what I had to say; he seated himself—on a sofa, near the embrasure of a window—motioned me to bring a chair to his side, and heard me in an erect attitude of thoughtful attention, re-assuring me now and then by reaching out to lay a hand on my knee when he saw from my hesitancy that I feared I might be too candid in my confidences; and the look of his eye and the touch of his hand were as if he said: "I'm your friend. Anything you may say is perfectly safe with me."

I told him of my father's imprisonment. "It is dreadful," he said. "You shock me to the soul." He spoke of their friendship, of his admiration for my father's work in Congress, of his personal regard for the man himself. "Of course," he said, "I have no sympathy with your peculiar marriage system, and I'll never be able to understand how a man like your father could enter it." I reminded him that my father believed it a system revealed and ordained by God. "I know," he replied. "That is what they say. And I suppose they have scriptural warrant for polygamy. But it is a thing that would be 'more honored in the breach than the observance.' Tell me, is the rule of the Church absolute over you younger men?"

I told him that it *was*, in respect of political control; that the situation in Utah had placed us where there was no possibility of compromise; that we must be of, with, and for our own people, or against them.

He asked me whether I intended to address myself to the President. I replied, "Not yet" —since the bills were still pending in Congress and were not being urged from the White House. He seemed pleased. As I afterwards learned, there was a strong rivalry between the President and the Secretary of State; and though I knew that Mr. Blaine's interest in Utah was almost wholly one of responsible statesmanship, warmed by a personal kindliness for our people, still it remains a fact that he expected the support of the Utah Republican delegation in the convention of 1892, and that it had been promised him by national Republicans who were now laboring at Washington in our behalf.

He encouraged me with an almost intimate emotion of pity and friendliness; and I felt the largeness of the man as much in the warmth of his humanity as in the breadth of his view. He approved of my appearing before the committees. "Go and tell them your own story, yourself," he said. "Make your plea independently of all the formal and official arguments that have been used. These have been exhausted. They have been ineffective. We must use the personal and"— he added it significantly—"the political appeal. If you find difficulty, let me know. I shall not be idle in your behalf. If you meet any insuperable obstacle, I'll see if I can't help you run over it."

He rose to terminate the interview. He looked at me with a smile. " 'The Lord giveth,' " he said, " 'and the Lord taketh away.' Wouldn't it be possible for your people to find some way—without disobedience to the commands of God—to bring yourselves into harmony with the law and institutions of this country? Believe me, it's *not* possible for any people as weak in numbers as yours, to set themselves up as superior to the majesty of a nation like this. We may succeed, this time, in preventing your disfranchisement; but nothing permanent can be done until you 'get into line.' "

He accompanied me toward the door, giving me friendly messages of regard to deliver to my father. He put his arm around my shoulders, at last, and said: "You may tell your father for me—as I tell you, young man— you shall not be harmed, *this* time."

I parted from him with an almost speechless relief and gratitude, and hurried to my father with the news of hope. I had not told Mr. Blaine that he was in Washington; for, without feeling that he saw himself marked by his imprisonment, I was aware that his friends might pity him for it, if they did not condemn him; and neither sentiment (I knew) was he of the personal temper to encounter.

I told him every detail of my talk with

the Secretary of State; he heard me, silently, meditatively. When I concluded with Mr. Blaine's assurance that we should not be harmed "this time," but must "get into line," he looked up at me with a significant steadiness of eye. "President Woodruff," he said, "has been praying. . . . He thinks he sees some light. . . . You are authorized to say that something will be done."

I asked no question. His gaze conveyed assurance, but forbade inquiry. I had to understand, without being told, that the Church was preparing to concede a recession from the doctrine of polygamy.

With this assurance to aid me, I began the work of reaching the committees—warm work in a Washington summer, but hopeful in the new prospect of a lasting success. The bill for disfranchisement had been reported out by the committees and was on the calendar for passage. It was necessary to have the question reopened before the committees for argument. In soliciting the opportunity of a re-hearing, from the Chairman of the Senate Committee, Senator Orville H. Platt, of Connecticut, I made my argument in a private conversation with him in his rooms in the Arlington Hotel. When I had done, he chewed his cigar a moment, looked at me quizically, and asked: "Do you know Abbot R. Heywood, of Ogden?"—and, as he asked it, he drew a letter from his pocket.

I replied that I knew Mr. Heywood well.

"I have a letter here from him, on this same subject," he said. "Tell me. What kind of man is he? And to what extent do you think I ought to depend on his views?"

I was never more tempted in my life to tell a lie. I knew Mr. Heywood to be a man of truth and high ideals; but he had been Chairman of the Anti-Church party in Weber County, and he had been one of the Gentile leaders for several years. I knew the intensity of his feelings against the rule of the Church in politics and the Mormon attitude of defiance to the law. I was sure that he would be strong in his demand for the passage of the disfranchisement act.

I hesitated a moment. Senator Platt was watching me. Then, with a resolve that our cause must stand or fall by the truth, I said: "Mr. Heywood is a man of integrity. I think he would write exactly what he believed to be true. But you know, Senator, intense feeling in politics sometimes sways a man's judgment. In view of Mr. Heywood's long controversy, I hope that if he has taken a view adverse to mine, his antagonism may be mitigated in your mind by your own knowledge of human feelings."

Senator Platt held out the letter to me. "You've won your motion for a re-hearing," he said. "I think we may be able to get the truth out of *you*. We have not always had it in this Utah question. Read that."

I read it. It was Mr. Heywood's solemn protest, as an American citizen—on behalf of himself and the other members of the perfunctory Republican Committee of his County—against the wholesale disfranchisement of the Mormons, on the ground that it would only delay a progressive American settlement of the territory!

Then I went to the other members of the Senate committee privately, and told them that the Mormon Church was about to make a concession concerning its doctrine of polygamy. I told them so in confidence, pointing out the necessity of secrecy, since to make public the news of such a recession, in advance, would be to prevent the Church from authorizing it. Not one of the Senators betrayed the trust. I was less confidential with the members of the House Committee, because I realized that nothing could be done against us unless the bill passed the Senate. But I gave the news of the Church's reconsideration of its attitude to Colonel G. W. R. Dorsey, the member from Nebraska, and he used his influence to get me a rehearing from the House Committee. Finally I appeared once before each committee, and argued our case at length. The bills did not become law. Aided by Mr. Blaine's powerful friendship, we were saved "for the time."

It remained to make our safety permanent, and I took train for Utah, on my father's counsel, to see President Woodruff. I had given my word that "something was to be done." I went to plead that it *should* be done—and done speedily.

CHAPTER IV

THE MANIFESTO

I found him in the office of the Presidency—in the little one-story house that I have described in my early interview with Joseph F. Smith—and he received me with the gracious affectionateness of a fatherly old man. He asked me, almost at once: "What are they going to do to us in Washington?"

"President Woodruff," I replied, "we've been spared—temporarily. The axe will not fall for a few moments. It depends on ourselves, now, whether it shall fall or not."

"Come into the other room," he said, under his voice, in an eager confidentiality, like a child with a secret. And pattering along ahead of me, quick on his feet, he signed to me to follow him—with little nods and beckonings—into the retiring room where I had talked with Smith.

There he sat down, on the edge of his chair, his elbows supported on the broad arms, leaning forward, partly bowed with his age, and partly with an intentness of curiosity that glittered innocently in his guileless eyes. A dear old character! Sweet in his sentiments, sweet in his language, sweet in the expression of his face.

I told him, in detail, of the events in Washington, and of the men who had helped us in them—particularly of Mr. Blaine, who was apparently a new character in his experience, and of Senator Orville H. Platt, in whom he discovered an almost neighborly interest when I told him that the Senator came from Connecticut, his native state. I warned him that the passage of the measure of disfranchisement had been no more than retarded. I pointed out the fatal consequences for the community if the bill should ever become law—the fatal consequences for the leaders of the Church if the non-polygamous Mormons, deprived of their votes, were ever left unable to control the administration of local government. I repeated the promise that my father had authorized me to carry to the Senators and Congressmen who still had the Cullom-Struble bill in hand; and I emphasized the fact that because of this promise the bill had been held back—with the certainty that it would never become law if we met the nation half way.

I was watching him to see if he sensed the point I wished him to get. When I touched the matter of my father's promise, his face became softly reverent; and when I had done—looking at me without a trace of cunning in his benignity, with an expression, rather, of exalted innocence and faith,—he said: "Brother Frank, I have been making it a matter of prayer. I have wrestled mightily with the Lord. And I think I see some light."

In order that there might be no misunderstanding, I put into plainer words what I meant and what the prominent men in Washington had been led to look for: since, by a "revelation" of the Church we were ordered to give obedience to the government of the nation, and since we had exhausted all our legal defences, it was hoped that the Prophet, Seer, and Revelator of the Church would find a way, under the guidance of God, to bring our people into conformity with the law.

As he accepted this calmly, I added: "To be very plain with you, President Woodruff, our friends expect, and the country will insist, that the Church shall yield the practice of plural marriage."

His eyelids quivered a little, but he showed no other sign of flinching. I saw that the counsels of his advisers and the comfort that he had derived from his prayers had prepared him for an immolation that was more serious to him than any personal sacrifice that he could make. He said sadly: "I had hoped we wouldn't have to meet this trouble this way. You know what it means to our people. I had hoped that the Lord might open the minds of the people of this nation to the truth, so that they might be converted to the everlasting covenant. Our prophets have suffered like those of old, and I thought that the persecutions of Zion were enough—that they would bring some other reward than this." If I had been the bearer of a new edict of proscription, I think he could not have been more profoundly oppressed by the sense of his responsibility. "Did your father tell you," he asked, "that I had been seeking the mind of the Lord?"

I replied that he had.

He reflected silently. "I shall talk with you again about it," he said, at last. "I hope the Lord will make the way plain for his people."

I do not wish to idealize the polygamous relation—but in monogamy a man is not persecuted for his marriage, and sometimes he does not appreciate the tie. In polygamy, the men and women alike had been compelled to suffer on its account by the grim trials of the life itself and by the hatred of all civilization arrayed against it. They had grown to value their marriage system by what it had cost them. They had been driven by the contempt of the world to argue for its sanctity, to live up to their declarations, and to raise it in their esteem to what it professed to be, the celestial order that prevailed in the Heavens! I knew, as well as President

Woodruff did, the wrench it would give their hearts to have to abandon, at last, what they had so long suffered for.

In the days of anxious waiting that followed, I saw Joseph F. Smith and sounded him for any hint of progress. He said: "I'm sure I don't know what can be done. Your father talked with President Woodruff and me before he went to Washington, but I'm sure I can't see how *we* can do anything." When my father returned home, I went to him many times—without however learning anything definite. I knew that the men in Washington would demand some tangible evidence of our good faith before Congress should reconvene; and I repeatedly urged the necessity of action.

At length he sent me word, in Ogden, that President Woodruff wished to confer with me, and he suggested that it would be permissible for me to speak my opinions freely. I hastened to Salt Lake City, to the offices of the Presidency. President Woodruff took me into a private room and read me his "manifesto."

It was the same that was issued on September 24, 1890, and ratified by a General Conference of the Mormon Church on October 6, following. It was the proclamation that freed the oppressed of Utah; for, by the subsequent "covenant"—and its acceptance by the Federal government—the nation did but confirm their freedom and accord them their constitutional rights. Here, shaking in the hand of age, was a sheet of paper by which the future of a half million people was to be directed; and that simple old man was to speak through it, to them, with the awful authority of the voice of God.

He told me he had written it himself, and it certainly appeared to me to be in his handwriting. Its authorship has since been variously attributed. Some of the present-day polygamists say that it was I who wrote it. Chas. W. Penrose and George Reynolds have claimed that they edited it. I presume that as Mormons, "in good standing," believing in the inspiration of the Prophet, they appreciate the blasphemy of their claim!

I found it disappointingly mild. It denied that the Church had been solemnizing any plural marriages of late, and advised the faithful "to refrain from contracting any marriages forbidden by the law of the land." In spite of this mildness, President Woodruff asked me whether I thought the Mormons would support the revelation—whether they would accept it.

I replied that there could be no proper anxiety on that point. The majority of the Mormon people were ready for such a message. It might be very much stronger without arousing resistance. With the exception of the comparatively few men and women who were living in polygamy, the community would accept it gratefully. Rather, I made bold to say, my anxiety was as to whether the nation would believe that such an equivocally-worded document meant an absolute recession from the practice of plural marriage.

It was plain that his advisers had not pointed out this danger to him. He asked me how I thought the nation would take it.

I asked him, point blank, whether it meant an absolute recession from polygamy.

He answered that it did.

Then (I said) with such an interpretation of it, and a formal and public acceptance of it by the Church authorities, I did not doubt that we could convince the nation of its sufficiency. I reminded him—as I am now glad to remember—that the word of the Mormon people had passed current in the political and commercial circles of the country; that I had several times been the bearer of messages from them to prominent men; that we had been taken on faith and the faith had been always vindicated. Finally, in order that I might carry away no misapprehension, nor convey any, I asked him if it was the intention of the manifesto to inhibit any further plural marriage living.

He answered, quaintly: "Why, of course, Frank—because that's what they've been persecuting us for." There was not even a shrewdness in his voice when he added: "You know they didn't get our brethren in prison for polygamy, but for living with their plural wives."

Perhaps no other man in Utah could have said such a thing without sarcasm. The fact was that the United States authorities had been practically unable to prove a case of polygamy (which was a felony) because the marriage records were concealed by the Church; but they could prove plural marriage living (a mere misdemeanor) by repute and circumstance. It was part of President Woodruff's unworldliness that he did not see the satire of his words; and I was the more convinced of his good faith.

I was convinced also, by several of his remarks, that he had consulted with the Church's attorney, Mr. Franklin S. Richards; and while I trusted the President's unworldly faith, I trusted more the sagacity of his more worldly advisers. I began to see, with a sure hope, the beginning of the end of all our miseries.

Some days later I was summoned to attend a meeting of the Church authorities in the President's offices; and I knew that the test had come. The Church was governed by the Presidency, composed of President Woodruff and his two Councillors, with the Quorum of the Twelve Apostles, the Presidents of Seventies, and the presiding Bishopric, composed of three members. These quorums aggregate twenty-five men; and to their number may be added the Chief Patriarch of the Church, making a body of twenty-six general authorities—the Hierarchy. It was from these latter men, polygamists and (I feared) parochial in their ignorance of the nation and their trust in the protection of their followers—it was from them (and the other practicers of polygamy) that any opposition would come to the acceptance and publication of the manifesto.

They met—something less than a score of them, with two or three of their most trusted advisers—in one of the general offices of the Presidency, sitting in leather chairs along its walls, with a sort of central skylight illuminating subduedly the anxiety of their silent faces. President Woodruff and his two Councillors entered to them; and this insignificant-looking apartment—of such tremendous community significance, because of the memories of its past—seemed to take on the gravity of another momentous crisis in the destiny of its people. The portraits in oils of the dead presidents, martyrs, and prophets of the Church, looked down on us from the façade of a little gallery, and caught my eyes almost hypnotically with the imperturbability of their gaze. No word from them! In the midst of the broken utterance of emotion—when the tears were wet on faces to whose manliness tears were the very sweat of martyrdom—I saw those immovable countenances as placid as the features of the dead.

President Woodruff stood under them, so old and other-worldly, that he seemed already of their circle rather than ours; and he spoke in a voice of feeling for us, but with a simple and courageous finality that sounded the very note of fate. He had called the brethren together (he said) to submit a decision to their consideration, and he desired from them an expression of their willingness to accept and abide by it. He knew what a trial it would be to the "whole household of Israel." "We have sought," he said, "to live our religion—to harm no one—to perform our mission in this world for the salvation of the living and the dead. We have obeyed the principle of celestial marriage because it came to us from God. We have suffered under the rage of the wicked; we were driven from our homes into the desert; our prophets have been slain, our holy ones persecuted—and it *did* seem to me that we were entitled to the constitutional protection of the courts in the practice of our religion."

But the courts had decided "against us." The great men of the nation were determined to show us no mercy. Legislation was impending that would put us "in the power of the wicked." Brother George Q. Cannon, Brother John T. Caine, and the other brethren who had been in Washington, had found that the situation of the Church was critical. Brother Franklin S. Richards had advised him that our last legal defence had fallen. "In broken and contrite spirit" he had sought the will of the Lord, and the Holy Spirit had revealed to him that it was necessary for the Church to relinquish the practice of that principle for which the brethren had been willing to lay down their lives.

A sort of ghastly stillness accepted what he said as a confirmation of the worst fears of the men who had evidently come there with some knowledge of what they were to hear. I glanced at the faces of those opposite me. A set and staring pallor held them motionless. I was conscious of a chill of heart that seemed communicated to me from them. My brother Abraham was sitting beside me; I knew his deep affection for his family; I knew with what a clutch of misery this edict of separation was crushing his hope; I felt myself growing as pale and tense as he.

The silence was broken by President Woodruff asking one of the brethren to read the manifesto. When it was concluded, he said: "The matter is now before you. I want you to speak as the Spirit moves you."

There was no reply, except a sort of general gasp of low-voiced interjections and a little buzz of whisperings that sounded like emotion taking its breath. He called on my father to speak. The First Councillor rose to make a statesmanlike review of the crisis; and I understood that with his usual diplomacy he was putting aside from him the authority of leadership until he could see whether an opposition was to develop that should make it necessary for him to front it.

That opposition made a rustle of stirring in the pause that followed. I saw it in the changed expressions of some of the faces. Several of the men—including my brother Abraham, and Joseph F. Smith—asked whether the manifesto meant a cessation of plural marriages: whether no more such marriages were to be allowed.

President Woodruff answered that it did; that the Lord had taken back the principle from the children of men and that we would have no power to restore it.

Then they asked whether it meant a cessation of plural marriage living—whether they would be required to separate from the wives whom they had taken in the holy covenant.

He answered, firmly, that it did; that the brethren in Washington found it imperative; that it was the will of the Lord; that we must submit.

I saw their faces flush and then slowly pale again—and the storm broke. One after another they rose and protested, hoarsely, in the voice of tears, that they were willing to suffer "persecution unto death" rather than to violate the covenants which they had made "in holy places" with the women who had trusted them. One after another they offered themselves for any sacrifice but this betrayal of the women and children to whom they owed an everlasting faith. And a manlier lot of men never spoke in a manlier way. Not a petty word was uttered. Their thought was not for themselves. Their grief was not selfish. Their protests had a dignity in pathos that shook me in spite of myself.

When they had done, my father rose again with a face that seemed to bear the marks of *their* grief while it repressed his own. He dwelt anew on the long efforts of our attorney and our friends in Congress to resist what we believed to be unconstitutional measures to repress our practice of a religious faith. But we were citizens of a nation. We were required to obey its laws. And when we found, by the highest judicial interpretation of statute and constitution, that we were without grounds for our plea of religious immunity, we had but the alternative either of defying the power of the whole nation or of submitting ourselves to its authority. For his part he was willing to do the will of the Lord. And since the Prophet of God, after a long season of prayer, had submitted this revelation as the will of the Lord, he was ready for the sacrifice. The leaders of the Church had no right to think of themselves. They must remember how loyally the people had sacrificed their substance and risked their safety to guard their brethren who were living in plural marriage. Those brethren must not be ungrateful now. They must not now refuse to make their sacrifice, in answer to the sacrifices that had been made for them so often. The people had long protected them. Now they must protect the people.

Under the commanding persuasion of his voice I saw the determination of their resistance begin to falter and relax. President Woodruff called on me to speak, and I felt that it was my duty to represent the needs, the hopes, and the opportunities of the hundreds of thousands of the undistinguished mass who would make no decision for themselves, but whose fate was trembling on the event. I rose to speak for them, with my hand on my brother's shoulder, knowing that my every word would be a stab at his heart, and hoping that my grasp might be a touch of sympathy to him—knowing that I must urge these elders to sacrifice themselves and their families for a redemption of which I was to share the benefits—but sustained by the remembrance of the solemn pledge which I had been authorized to give in Washington to honorable men who had trusted in our honor—and strengthened by the thought of all those dear to me, whose sufferings would be multiplied, with no hope of relief, if the few would not now yield to save the many.

I described the situation as I had seen it in Washington and as I knew it in Utah from a more intimate personal experience than these leaders could have of the sufferings of the people. I told them how cheerfully and bravely the non-polygamists had borne the brunt of protecting them in the practice of their faith, and yet how patient a hope had been always with us that the final demand might not be made upon us for the sacrifice of a citizenship which we valued more because it shielded them than because it armed us.

Encouraged by the face of President Woodruff, I reminded them that the sorrow and the parting, at which they rebelled, could only be for a little breath of time, according to their faith; that by the celestial covenant, into which they had entered, they were assured that they should have their wives and children with them throughout the endless ages of eternity. The people had given much to them. Surely *they* could yield the domestic happinesses of the little remaining day of life in this world, in order to save and prosper those who were not to enjoy *their* supreme exaltation of beatitude in the world to come.

I had felt my brother strong under my hand. He rose, when I concluded. And with a manful brevity he replied that he submitted because it was the will of the Lord, and because he had no right to interpose his selfish love and yearnings between the people

of God and their worldly opportunity. The
others followed. Not one referred to the
equivocal language of the manifesto or ques-
tioned it. They accepted it—as it was then
and afterwards interpreted—as a revelation
from God made through the Prophet of the
Church; and they subscribed to it as a solemn
covenant, before God, with the people of the
nation.

Joseph F. Smith was one of the last to
speak. With a face like wax, his hands out-
stretched, in an intensity of passion that
seemed as if it must sweep the assembly, he
declared that he had covenanted, at the altar
of God's house, in the presence of his Father,
to cherish the wives and children whom the
Lord had given him. They were more to
him than life. They were dearer to him than
happiness. He would rather choose to stand,
with them, alone—persecuted—proscribed—
outlawed—to wait until God in His anger
should break the nation with His avenging
stroke. But—

He dropped his arms. He seemed to shrink
in his commanding stature like a man stricken
with a paralysis of despair. The tears came
to the pained constriction of his eyelids.

"I have never disobeyed a revelation from
God," he said. "I cannot—I dare not—
now."

He announced—with his head up, though
his body swayed—that he would accept and

abide by the revelation. When he sank in his chair and covered his face with his hands, there was a gasp of sympathy and relief, as if we had been hearing the pain of a man in agony. And my heart gave a great leap; for, in these supreme moments of feeling, things come to us that are larger than our knowledge, more splendid than our hopes; and I saw, as if in the blinding glisten of the tears in my eyes, a radiant vision of our future, an unselfish people freed from a burden of persecution, a nation's forgiveness born, a grateful state created. I saw it—and I looked at Smith and loved him for it. I knew then, as I know now, that he and those others were at this moment sincere. I knew that they had relinquished what was more dear to them than the breath of life. I knew the appalling significance, to them, of the promise which they were making to the nation. And in all the degraded after-years, when so many of them were guilty of breach of covenant and base violation of trust, I tried never to forget that in the hour of their greatest trial, they had sacrificed themselves for their people; they had suffered for the happiness of others; they had said, sincerely: "Not my will, O Lord, but Thine, be done!"

CHAPTER V

ON THE ROAD TO FREEDOM

In any discussion of the public affairs that make the subject matter of this narrative, a line of discrimination must be drawn at the year 1890. In that year the Church began a progressive course of submission to the civil law, and the nation received each act of surrender with forgiveness. The previous defiances of the Mormon people ceased to give grounds for a complaint against them. The old harshnesses of the Federal government were cancelled by the new generosity of a placated nation. And neither party to the present strife in Utah should go back, beyond the period of this composition, to dig up, from the past, its buried wrongs.

In relating, here, some of the events of 1888 and 1889, I have tried neither to justify the Mormons nor to defend their prosecutors. I have wished merely to make clear the situation in Utah, and to introduce to you, in advance, some of the leaders of the distracted community, so that you might understand the conditions from which the Mormons escaped by giving their covenant to the nation and be able to judge of the obligations and responsibilities of the men who gave it.

I have described the promulgation and acceptance of "the manifesto" with such circumstance and detail, because of what has since occurred in Utah. Let me add that some two weeks later the General Conference of the Church endorsed the President's pronouncement as "authoritative and binding." And let me point out that it was the first and only law of the Mormon Church ever so sustained by triple sanctities—"revealed" as a command from God, accepted by the prophets in solemn fraternity assembled, and ratified by the vote of the entire "congregation of Israel" before it was declared to be binding upon men.

At first, because of the somewhat indefinite promise of the message itself, many of the non-Mormons of Utah remained suspicious and in doubt of it. But it was recognized by Judge Zane, in court—on the day following the close of the Conference—as an official declaration, "honest and sincere." The newspapers throughout the whole country so received it. The Church authorities sent assurances to Washington that convinced the statesmen, there, of the completeness and finality of the submission. And the good faith of the covenant was at last admitted by the non-Mormons of Utah and endorsed by their trust. I do not know of any change in human affairs—dependent on human will—more speedy, effective and comprehensive than this recession. Within the space of a few days a revolution was completed that had been sought by the power of our nation and of the civilized world, for a generation, with stripes and imprisonment, death, confiscation and the ostracism of the country's public contempt. It had been obtained, I knew, chiefly by the sagacity of the First Councillor using the pressure of circumstances to enforce the persuasions of diplomacy. I felt that a miracle of change had been brought to pass. He had placed us on the road to freedom; and I trusted his guidance to lead us to our goal.

That goal, to me personally, was the honor of American citizenship—an ambition that had been an obsession with me from my earliest youth. I had never heard a man on a railroad train talk of how he was going to vote in a national election, without feeling a pang of shamed envy; for my lack of citizenship seemed a mark of inferiority. The patriotic reading of my boyhood had made the American republic, to me, the noblest administration of freemen in the history of government and the exercise of its franchise literally the highest dignity of human privilege. I would have been as proud—I *was* as proud when the day came—to vote for the President of the United States as he could have been to take his oath of office. I do not believe that any poor serf, escaped from

114

the tyranny of Russia, ever saw the American shore with a more grateful eye than I looked to the prospect of being admitted, with the citizens of Utah, into the enfranchisement of the Republic.

But it was evident that the Church's recession from polygamy would not be enough to free us, so long as its control of politics remained. Its other practices had flourished and been sheltered under its political power; and now that the Church had ceased to be a lawbreaker, our friends in Washington were properly expecting that it would cease to interfere with its members in the exercise of their citizenship. For this reason, when I was notified that I had been selected as a member of the advisory committee of the People's Party (the Church party), I went at once to my father and told him that I would not take the place; that I intended to work, personally, and through my newspaper, for the political division of Utah on the lines of the national parties. He held that until Gentile solidarity was dissolved, it would be dangerous to divide the allegiance of the Mormons; but he did not stand against my protest; he contented himself—diplomatically—with sending me to consult with President Woodruff and Joseph F. Smith.

To them, I argued that the political emancipation of the Mormon people from ecclesiastical direction was as necessary as the recession from polygamy had been. We must be set free to perform our duty to the country solely as citizens of the country, before we could expect to be given the right to perform it at all. And, for my part, the only action I would consent to take as a member of the advisory committee of the People's Party would be to vote for the dissolution of the party.

President Woodruff referred me to my father, and advised me to be guided by him. Joseph F. Smith urged that a division of the Mormon people on national party lines would enable the Liberal (the Gentile) party to march in between. I argued in reply that we must divide at some time, and the sooner the better, since every year was increasing the Gentile population. They would never split as long as we remained solid. And if we were ever to be permitted to nationalize ourselves, it would not be until we had dissolved the party organizations whose very names were a proof of the continued rule of the Church in politics.

When he had no more arguments to advance, he gave a reluctant assent to mine. I reported back to my father and he approved of my plans. He asked me humorously with whom I expected to affiliate, since he knew of no one who was likely to go with me; but I could see that he was pleased with my independence and hoped I might succeed in doing something to break the deadlock-grapple of Mormon and Gentile that held Utah apart from the rest of the country in politics.

His humorous idea of my undertaking gave its color to my beginnings. It was rather a spirited adventure, as I look back upon it now. When we organized a Republican Club at Ogden, my intimate friend, Ben E. Rich, and another friend named Joseph Belnap, were the only Mormons, so far as I know, who joined me in becoming members. Outside of us three, I did not know of another Mormon Republican in the whole territory.

Indeed, the status of the Mormon people, in their fancied relation to the two great parties of the country, was almost identical with that of the people of the South after the Civil War. Practically every Mormon believed himself to be a Democrat. Among the young men of the Church there had been occasional attempts to form Democratic Clubs. Mr. John T. Caine, delegate in Congress from the territory, was a Democrat. My father had sat on the Democratic side of the House. Almost all the men who had braved the sentiments of their own states, to speak for us in Congress, had been Democrats. And, of course, the administration of the laws that had been so cruel to the feelings of the Mormons had been in Republican hands.

117

Two years earlier, in Ogden, I had spoken in a meeting of Republicans that had been called to rejoice over the election of Benjamin Harrison to the Presidency; and I was still being taunted by my Mormon friends with having clasped hands with "the persecutors of the Prophets." When I came out, now, as an advocate of Republicanism, I was met everywhere with this charge—that I had joined the enemies of the Church, that I was assisting the persecutors of my father. The fact that my father approved of what I was doing, relieved the seriousness of the situation for me; and the humorous assistance of Ben Rich in our political evangelism gave a secret chuckle to many of the incidents of our campaign.

We went from town to town, from district to district, up the mountain valleys, across the plains, into mining camps and farming communities—using the meeting-houses, the school-rooms, the town halls—taking the afternoon to coax the tired workers of the fields or of the mines to come and hear us in the evening, and watching them fall asleep in the light of our borrowed kerosene lamps while we talked. They came eagerly. Indeed, my own ambition for citizenship—for a right to participate in the affairs of the nation—was probably no keener than theirs; and they had an innocent curiosity about the questions of national politics, of which they

UNDER THE PROPHET IN UTAH

had never before been invited to know anything. They listened almost devoutly.

"Brethren and sisters," a bishop exhorted
them at a meeting in which one of our party
was to speak, "we have come to listen to this
man, and I hope we will be guided in all our
reflections by the Spirit of God and that we
will do nothing to offend that Spirit. Let
there be no commotion, no whispering, and,
above all, no hand clapping."

In a life that had as few diversions as theirs,
a political meeting was an exciting event.
The whole family came, and the mothers
brought their babies. Surely in no other
American community did politics ever have
such a homely and serious consideration.
Certainly no other community would have
so quickly understood the theories of the two
parties or accepted them so implicitly.

But it was all theory! I recognize, now,
that I preached a Republicanism that was
an ideal of what it should be, rather than any
modern faith of the "practical politician."
I had gathered it from my reading, from hearing the speeches in Congress, from sympathetic
conferences with the great men who were
responsible for the dogmas of the party; and
every assurance of grace that their ability
could give and my credulity accept, I proclaimed religiously as a political salvation
to our people. I built up an ideal, and then
judged the party thereafter according to the

measure of that ideal. When I found that some of the charges against the Republican party were true—charges which I had indignantly repelled—I was as shocked as any pious worshipper who ever found that his idol had feet of clay. Our people, having accepted the faith with as simple a hope as it was offered, were as easily turned from it when they found that it was false. The political moods of Utah, for its first few years of statehood, were a puzzle to the "practical" leaders of the parties; but to us who understood the impulses of honesty that moved the changes, things were as clear as they were encouraging.

During the previous summer in Washington, I had met General James S. Clarkson, then president of the National League of Republican Clubs; and now, on his invitation, in the Spring of 1891, Rich and I went to Louisville to speak before the national convention of the league. Through the kindness of General Clarkson, I was given the official recognition of a perfunctory place on the executive committee of the league's national committee, and came into touch with many of the party leaders. It was about this time, I imagine, that they conceived the idea of using the gratitude of the Mormons in order to carry Utah and the surrounding states in which the Mormon vote might constitute a balance of political power. I know

that the idea was old and established when
I came upon it, in 1894, during the campaign
for statehood. As I also found, still later,
the Republican leaders and the business interests with which they were in relation, had
their eyes on a distant prospect of fabulous
financial schemes in which the secret funds
of the Church were to help in the building of
railroads and the promoting of other enterprises of associated capital. But at the time
of which I am writing, I had not had sufficient
experience to suspect the motives of the men
who encouraged our work in Utah; and I
accepted in good faith their public declarations
that the sole aim of the party was to serve
the needs of the people of the United States—
and therefore of the people of Utah!

It seemed to me that such a noble principle
should win the support of Mormon and Gentile
alike, and it was on this principle that I appealed for the support of both. I was so sure
of winning with it that I resented and fought
against the aid of the Church that came to
us as our campaign succeeded.

The People's Party (the Church Party) had
been dissolved (June, 1891) by the formal
action of the executive committee, under
the direct instruction of the leaders of the
Church. The tendency was for its members
to organize themselves immediately as a
Democratic party. They were led by such
brilliant and trusted defenders of the Church

as Franklin S. Richards, Chas. C. Richards, Wm. H. King, James H. Moyle, Brigham H. Roberts and Apostle Moses Thatcher; and a group of abler advocates could not have been found in any state in the Union. It was against the sentiment of the Mormon people, vivified by such inspiring Democracy as these men taught, that our little organization of Republicans had to make headway; and an anxiety began to show itself among the Church authorities for a less unequal division, and consequently a greater appearance of political independence, among the faithful.

Apostle John Henry Smith came out as a Republican stump speaker in rivalry with Moses Thatcher, the Democratic Prophet. Joseph F. Smith announced himself a Republican descendant of Whigs. Apostle Francis Marion Lyman, in his religious ministrations, counselled leading brethren to withhold themselves from the Democratic party unless they had gone too far to retreat. Men of ecclesiastical office in various parts of the territory— who were regarded as being safe in their wisdom and fidelity—were urged to hold themselves and their influence in reserve for such use on *either* side of politics as the future might demand.

Against this ecclesiastical direction of the people's choice, I objected again and again to the Presidency, and my objections seemed to meet with acquiescence. It required no prescience on my part to foresee that the growing dislike and distrust of Moses Thatcher at Church headquarters would lead to a strife in the Church that might be carried into our politics; and I knew how small would be the hope of preserving any political independence, if once it were involved in the intrigues of priests and their rivalries for a supremacy of influence among the people. I was resolved that not even a Church, ruling by "divine right," should interpose between my country and my franchise; and an encroachment that I would not permit upon my own freedom, I would not help to inflict upon others.

The men with whom I had been working proposed me as the candidate for Congress of the new Utah Republicans; and I was supported by a strong delegation from my own country and from other parts of the territory; but I found that I was not "satisfactory" to some of the Mormon leaders, and in the convention (1892) Apostle John Henry Smith and my cousin George M. Cannon led in an attempt to nominate Judge Chas. Bennett, a Gentile lawyer. After a bitter fight of two days and nights, we carried the convention against them, and I was nominated.

The Democrats selected, as their candidate, one of the strongest characters in the territory, Joseph L. Rawlins. He was the son of a Mormon bishop, but he had left the Church immediately upon reaching manhood. He was a great lawyer, a staunch Democrat, and wonderfully popular. There followed one of the swiftest and most exciting campaigns ever seen in Utah. The whole people rose to it with enthusiasm. Our party chairman, Chas. Crane, had a genius for organization; our speakers drew crowded meetings; and though charges of Church influence were made by both sides, the question of religion was no longer the one that divided Utah.

We were getting on famously, when an incident occurred that was at once disastrous and salutary. While I was away from headquarters, stumping the districts, Chairman Crane (who was a Gentile), Ben Rich and Joseph F. Smith, issued a pamphlet in Republican behalf called "Nuggets of Truth." It gave a picture of Joseph Smith, the original Prophet, on the first page and a picture of me on the last one. (They issued also a certificate, obtained by Joseph F. Smith and given out by him, that I was a Mormon "in good standing.") As soon as I heard of the matter, I wired Chairman Crane that unless the pamphlet were immediately withdrawn, I should return to Salt Lake City and publicly denounce such methods. It was withdrawn, but the damage was done, I was defeated, as I deserved to be—though I was the innocent victim of the atrocity—and Mr. Rawlins was elected.

The campaign proved, however, that if the Church leaders would only keep their hands off, there was ample strength in either party to make a presentation of national issues of sufficient appeal to divide the people on party lines; and it was evident that the people would choose the party that made the best showing of principles and candidates. "Nuggets of Truth" left us with a nasty sense that at no hour were we assured of safety from ecclesiastical interference—or the nefarious attempt to make an appearance of such interference—in our political affairs. But the disaster that followed, in this instance, was so prompt that we could hope it would prove a lesson.

Most important of all, the campaign had made it evident that there was now no political mission in Utah for the Liberal (the Gentile) party—assuming that the retirement of the Mormon priests from politics was sincere and permanent. Accordingly, the organization formally met some months later, and formally dissolved; and, by that act, the last great obstacle to united progress was removed from our road to statehood, and the men who removed it acted with a generosity that makes one of the noblest records of self-sacrifice in the history of the state.

They could foresee that their dissolution as a separate force meant statehood for Utah— a sovereignty in itself that would leave the

Gentiles in the minority and without any appeal to the nation. Under territorial conditions, although the non-Mormons were less than one-third of the population, they had two-thirds of the political power. They held all the Federal offices, including executive and judicial positions. They had the Governor, with an absolute veto over the acts of the Mormon legislature. They had the President and Congress who could annul any statute of the territory; and they had with them almost the entire sentiment of the nation. It was in their power to have protracted the Mormon controversy, and to have withstood the appeal for statehood, to this day.

They yielded everything; they accepted, in return, only the good faith of the Mormons. Was it within the capacity of any human mind to foresee that in return for such generosity the Church would ever give over its tabernacles to teaching its people to hold in detestation the very names of these men who saved us? Was it to be suspected that the political power surrendered by them would ever be used as a persecution upon them?— that the liberty, given by them *to* us, would ever afterward be denied them *by* us? It was inconceivable. Neither in the magnanimity of their minds nor in the gratitude of ours was there a suspicion of such a catastrophe.

During 1891, President Woodruff's manifesto had been ratified in local Church conferences in every "stake of Zion;" and a second General Conference had endorsed it in October of that year. President Woodruff, Councillor Joseph F. Smith and Apostle Lorenzo Snow went before the Federal Master in Chancery—in a proceeding to regain possession of escheated Church property—and swore that the manifesto had prohibited plural marriages, that it required a cessation of all plural marriage living, and that it was being obeyed by the Mormon people. These facts were recited in a petition for amnesty forwarded to President Harrison in December, 1891, accompanied by signed statements from Chief Justice Zane, Governor Thomas and other non-Mormons who pledged themselves that the petitioners were sincere and that if amnesty were granted good faith would be kept. "Our people are scattered," President Woodruff and his apostles declared in their petition. "Homes are made desolate. Many are still imprisoned; others are banished and in hiding. Our hearts bleed for these. In the past they followed our counsels, and while they are still afflicted our souls are in sackcloth and ashes. . . . As shepherds of a patient and suffering people we ask amnesty for them and pledge our faith and honor for their future."

At Washington, the Church's attorney, Mr. Franklin S. Richards, and delegate John T. Caine supported the petition with their avowals of the sincerity of the Church leaders, the genuineness of our political division, and the sanctity with which we regarded the promise to obey the laws. The Utah Commission, a non-Mormon body, favored amnesty in an official report of September, 1892. And when I went to Washington, in the winter of 1892–3, the changed attitude of the Federal authorities toward us was strikingly evident.

President Harrison issued his amnesty proclamation, early in January, 1893, to all persons liable to the penalties of the Edmunds-Tucker Act, but "on the express condition that they shall in the future faithfully obey the laws of the United States . . . and not otherwise." The proclamation concluded: "Those who fail to avail themselves of the clemency hereby offered will be vigorously prosecuted." Not a polygamist in Utah, to my knowledge, declined to take advantage of the mercy, by refusing the expressly implied pledge.

Meanwhile the campaign had been continued for the return of the escheated Church property and for the passage of an Enabling Act that should permit the territory to organize for statehood.* Joseph L. Rawlins,

---

*Statehood seemed still very far away. There was a Trans-Mississippi Congress held at Ogden in 1892, and though the delegates—coming from all the states and territories "west of the river,"—were the guests of the people of Utah, so hopeless was our status in the consideration of mankind that the delegates from the territories of New Mexico and Arizona

Democratic delegate from Utah, worked valiantly among the Democrats, and he was assisted by the influence of Mr. Franklin S. Richards and John T. Caine and others among their old associates in that party. But, in the very midst of the fight, we were advised that, unless the Republican leaders would let the Enabling Act go through, the Democratic leaders would falter in our advocacy.

I had been urged to go to Washington by the Presidency to do what I might to allay Republican antagonism, and I found that a number of self-appointed lobbyists (who expected political preferments and other rewards from the Church in the event of statehood) had been using the most amazing arguments in our behalf. For example, they told some of the "financial Senators" that the Church had fourteen million dollars in secret funds with which to help build a railroad to the coast as soon as statehood should be granted. They cited the number of the Church's adherents in all the states and terri-

would not let our names be joined to theirs in a resolution for statehood which we wished the committee on resolutions to propose to the Congress. Governor Prince of New Mexico replied, to our plea for a share in the resolution, that he did not intend to damn New Mexico by having her mixed up with Utah. We appealed to the Congress, and we were saved by a speech made by Thos. M. Patterson of Colorado, subsequently senator from Colorado, who carried the day for us. At a recent Trans-Mississippi Congress held in Denver, I sat with ex-Senator Patterson to hear Mr. Prince still proposing resolutions in support of statehood for New Mexico. Twenty years later!

129

tories of the Pacific Coast and as far east as Iowa and Missouri, and predicted that the gratitude of these people to the Republicans who were helping to free Utah would enable the Republican party to control a balance of political power in the several states. They declared positively that plural marriages and plural marriage living had utterly ceased among the Mormons for all time. And they made such statements with great particularity to Senator Orville H. Platt, of Connecticut, who was too wise a man to credit them.

As soon as I returned to Washington, he summoned me to a private meeting, in his parlor in the Arlington Hotel, and confronted me with one of the Republican lobbyists who had been soliciting his personal favor and his almost controlling influence. "Now, Mr. Cannon," he said, in his dry way, "have the Mormons stopped living with their plural wives? And will there never be another case of plural marriage among them?"

I remembered the lesson of my interview with him at the time of the campaign against the disfranchisement bill, and I answered: "No. Not all the men of the Church have complied fully with the law. So far as I know, all the general authorities of the Church— with two or three exceptions—are fulfilling the covenant they gave; and so far as I can judge there will never be another plural marriage ceremony with the consent or con-

nivance of the leaders of the Church. But
human nature is very much the same in Utah
as it is in Connecticut. Here and there, no
doubt, a man feels that he's under an obligation to keep his covenant with his plural
wives in preference to the covenant of his
accepted amnesty; and there and here, possibly, in the future, some man will break the
law and defy the orders of the Church and
take a plural wife. But the leaders of the
Church do not countenance either proceeding,
and any man who violates the law, in either
respect, offends against the revelations of the
Church and, I believe, will be dealt with as
an apostate. I come direct from the Presidency of the Church, and I am authorized
to pledge their word of honor that they will
themselves obey the law and do all in their
power as men and leaders to bring their people
into harmony with the institutions of this
country as rapidly as possible."

Senator Platt had slowly unwrapped him,
self, rising from his chair to his full height of
more than six feet, in a lank and alarming
indignation. "There," he said, striding up
and down the room. "That's it! That's
just it. These people have been telling us
that you were obeying the law—all of you—
in every instance—and would always obey it.
And now you come here and admit, openly,
that some of you, to whom we have granted
amnesty, are breaking your word—and that

'*possibly*' others, in the future, will do the same thing!"

"Senator," I pleaded, "what confidence could you have in me if I were to tell you the Mormons were so superhuman that in a single day they could eliminate all their human characteristics? I'm asking you to recognize that the tendency imparted to a whole community is more important than any one man's breach of the law. Believe me, if you grant us our statehood, there will never be any lawbreaking *sanctioned* or protected by the Church leaders, and just as speedily as possible the entire system will be brought into harmony with the institutions of the nation. I'm telling you the truth."

He turned on me to ask, abruptly, how the polygamists had adjusted their family affairs.

I answered that in nearly all cases within my personal knowledge, the polygamist had relinquished conjugal relations with his plural wives with the full acquiescence of them and their children. He supported them, cared for the children, and in all other ways acted as the guardian and protector of the household. In a few cases men had gone to an extreme. For instance, my uncle, Angus M. Cannon—president of the Salt Lake "stake of Zion," a man of most decided character—had declared that he had entered into his marriage relations with his wives under a

132

covenant that gave them equality in his regards; and in order that he might not wound the sensibilities of any, he had separated himself from all.

I reminded Senator Platt that with such examples on the part of the leaders, there could be no general law-breaking among the Mormons, and that gradually the polygamous element would accommodate itself to the demands of law and the commands of God.

He waved us away with a curt announcement that he would have to think the matter over. If I had not known the essential justice and common sense under his dry and irascible exterior, I might have been alarmed. The lobbyist's concern was almost comic. As soon as we were out of hearing of the Senator's apartment, shaking both fists frantically at me, he cried: "You've ruined everything! We had him. We had him—all right—until you came down here and let the cat out of the bag! You *knew* what we'd been telling him. Why didn't you stick to it?"

I replied with equal warmth: " *You* may lie all you please; but if we have to win Utah's statehood with lies I don't want it. Senator Platt has been generous to us in our time of need, and I don't intend to deceive him—or any other man."

As a matter of fact, this was not only common honesty; it was also the best policy. Senator Platt was, from that time to the day of his death, a good friend and wise counsellor of the people of Utah. And I wish to lay particular stress upon this conversation with him, because it was a type of many had with such men as he. Fred T. Dubois, delegate in Congress from the territory of Idaho and subsequently Senator from that state, had been perhaps the strongest single opponent, in Washington, of the Mormon Church; he took our promises of honor, as Senator Platt did, and he pacified Senator Cullom, Senator Pettigrew and many others among our antagonists, who afterwards told me that they had accepted the pledges given by Senator Dubois in our behalf.

They recognized that the Church and the community ought not to be held responsible for a few possible cases of individual resistance or offence, so long as there should be a strict adherence by the Church and its leaders to their personal and community covenant. I emphasize the nature of this generous appreciation of our difficulties, because the present-day polygamists in Utah claim that there was a "tacit understanding," between the statesmen in Washington and the agents of the Church, to the effect that the polygamists of that time might continue to live with their plural wives. This is not true. There never was any such understanding, to my knowledge. And there could not have been one, in the circumstances, *without* my knowledge.

For though I did not know what delegate Rawlins, and former delegate Caine, and our attorney, Mr. Richards, were saying in their private interviews with senators and congressmen, I know that in all the frequent conversations I had with them I never heard an intimation of any "tacit understanding" beyond the one which I have defined.

For my part I was more than eager to have all our political disabilities removed, the Church property restored, and the right of statehood accorded—believing implicitly in the sincerity of the Mormon leaders. I knew President Woodruff too well to doubt the pellucid character of his mind and purpose. I knew from my father's personal assurance—and from his constant practice from that time to the day of his death—that he was acting in good faith. I knew that the community was gladly following where these men led. I saw no slightest indication that any reactionary policy was likely to be entered upon in Utah, or that our people would accept it if it *were*.

The Church's personal property was restored by an Act of Congress approved October 25, 1893, but it was stipulated in the Act that the money was not to be used for the support of any church buildings in which "the rightfulness of the practice of polygamy" should be taught. Similarly, when the Enabling Act was approved, in July 16, 1894, it, too, provided that "polygamous or plural marriage" was forever prohibited. A constitutional convention was held at Salt Lake City under the provisions of that act, and a constitution was adopted in which it was provided that "polygamous or plural marriages" were forever prohibited, that the territorial laws against polygamy were to be continued in force, that there should be "no union of church and state," and that no church should "dominate the state or interfere with its functions." Upon no other basis would the nation have granted us our statehood; and we accepted the grant, knowing the expressed condition involved in that acceptance.

But there was one other gift that came to us from the nation—by Congressional enactment and later by Utah statute as a consequence of statehood; and that gift was the legitimizing of every child born of plural marriage before January, 1896. The solemn benignity of the concession touched me, as it must have touched many, to the very heart of gratitude. By it, ten thousand children were taken from the outer darkness of this world's conventional exclusion and placed within the honored relations of mankind. It was a tribute to the purity and sincerity of the Mormon women who had borne the cross of plural marriage, believing that God had commanded their suffering. It recognized the holy nature and honorable intent of the marriages of these women, by according their children every right of legal inheritance from their fathers. If all other covenants could be forgotten and their proof obliterated, *this* should remain as Utah's pledge of honor— sacred for the sake of the Mormon mothers, holy in the name of the uplifted child.

CHAPTER VI

THE GOAL—AND AFTER

Here we were then (as I saw the situation) assured of our statehood, rid of polygamy, relieved of religious control in politics, and free to devote our energies to the development of the land and the industries and the business of the community. The persecutions that our people had borne had schooled them to co-operation. They were ready, helping one another, to advance together to a common prosperity. They were under the leadership chiefly of the man who had guided them out of a most desperate condition of oppression toward the freedom of sovereign self-government. In that progress he had saved everything that was worthy in the Mormon communism; he had discarded much that was a curse. I knew that he had no thought but for the welfare of the people; and with such a man, leading such a following, we seemed certain of a future that should be an example to the world.

But both the Church and the people had been involved in debt by confiscation and proscription; and it was necessary now to free ourselves financially. This work my father undertook in behalf of the Presidency —for the President of the Mormon Church is not only the Prophet, Seer and Revelator of God to the faithful; he is also "the trustee in trust" of all the Church's material property. He is the controller, almost the owner, of everything it owns. He is as sacred in his financial as in his religious absolutism. He is accountable to no one. The Church auditors, whom he appoints, concern themselves merely with the details of bookkeeping. The millions of dollars that are paid to him, by the people in tithes, are used by him as he sees fit to use them; and the annual contributors to this "common fund" would no more question his administration of it than they would question the ways of divinity.

In the early days there had been a strongly animating idea that among the divinely-authorized duties of leadership was the obligation to develop the natural resources of the country in order to meet the people's needs. As the immigrants poured into Utah, these needs increased; and the Church leaders used the Church funds to develop coal and iron mines, support salt gardens, build a railway, establish a sugar factory (for which the people, through the legislature, voted a bounty), conduct a beach resort, and aid a hundred other enterprises that promised to be for the public good. These undertakings were not financed for profit. They were semi-socialistic in their establishment and half-benevolent in their administration.

But during "the days of the raid" they were neglected, because the Church was involved in debt. And now it became pressingly necessary to obtain money to restore the moribund industries and to meet the payments that were continually falling due upon loans made to the Presidency. President Woodruff called on me to aid in the work. So I came into touch with a development of events that did not seem to me, then, of any great importance; yet it drew as its consequence a connection between the Mormon Church and the great financial "interests" of the East—a connection that is one of the strong determining causes of the perversion of government and denial of political liberty in Utah today.

I wish, here, simply to foreshadow this connection. It will reappear in the story again and again; and it is necessary to have the significance of the recurrence understood in advance. But, at the time of which I write, there was no more than an innocent approach on our part to Eastern financiers to obtain money for the Church and to concentrate our debts in the hands of two or three New York banks.

For example, the Church had loaned to, or endorsed for, the Utah Sugar Company to the amount of $325,000; and my father had personally endorsed the general obligations for this and other sums, although he owned only $5,000 of the company's stock. He supported the factory with his personal credit and assumed the risk of loss (without any corresponding possibility of gain) in order to benefit the whole people by encouraging the beet sugar industry. A vain attempt had been made to sell the bonds in New York. Finally, the Church bought all the bonds of the company for $325,000 (of a face value of $400,000), and we sold them, for the Church, to Mr. Joseph Bannigan, the "rubber king," of Providence, Rhode Island, for $360,000, with the guarantee of the First Presidency, the trustee of the Church, and myself.

Similarly, the First Presidency led in building an electric power plant in Ogden, after Chas. K. Bannister, a great engineer, and myself had persuaded the members of the Presidency that the work would benefit the community. The bonds of this company, too, were bought by Mr. Bannigan, with the guarantee of the trustee of the Church, the Presidency and myself. Both the power plant and the sugar factory were financially successful. They performed a large public service beneficently. The fact that Mr. Bannigan held their bonds was no detriment to their work and wrought no injury to the people.

I single out these two enterprises because Joseph F. Smith has since sold the power plant to the "Harriman interests," and the control of the sugar factory to the sugar trust; and he has explained that in making the sales he merely followed my father's example and mine in selling the bonds to Mr. Bannigan. The power plant is now a part of the merger called the Utah Light and Railway Company, which has a monopoly right in all the streets of Salt Lake City and its suburbs, besides owning the electric power and light plants of Salt Lake City and Ogden, the gas plants of both these cities, and the natural gas wells and pipe lines supplying them. The Mormon people whose tithes aided these properties— whose good-will maintained them—whose leaders designed them as a community work for a community benefit—these people are now being mercilessly exploited by the Eastern "interests" to whom the Prophet of the Church has sold them bodily. The difference between selling the bonds of the sugar company to Bannigan, in order to raise money to support the factory, and selling half the stock to the sugar trust, in order to make a monopoly profit out of the Mormon consumers of sugar, has either not occurred to Smith or has been divinely waived by him.

However, this is by the way and in advance of my story. In 1894 we had no more fear of the Eastern money power than we had of the return of the Church to politics or to polygamy. Throughout 1893 and 1894 I was engaged in the work of re-establishing the

Church's business affairs with my father and a sort of finance committee of which the other two members were Colonel N. W. Clayton, of Salt Lake City, and Mr. James Jack, the cashier of the Church. In the summer of 1894 I heard various rumors that when Utah should gain its statehood, my father would probably be a candidate for the United States Senate. Since this would be a palpable breach of the Church's agreement to keep out of politics, I took occasion—one day, on a railroad journey—to ask him if he intended to be a candidate.

He told me that he was being urged to stand for the Senatorship, but that for his part he had no desire to do so; and he asked me what I thought about it. I replied that if I had felt it was right for him to take the office and he desired it, I would walk barefoot across the continent to aid him. But I re-minded him of the pledges which he and I had made repeatedly—on our own behalf, in the name of his associates in leadership, and on the honor of the Mormon people—to subdue thereafter the causes of the controversy that had divided Mormon and Gentile in Utah. He replied with an emphatic assurance of his purpose to keep those pledges, and dismissed the subject with a finality that left no doubt in my mind.

I know that he might have desired the Sena-torship as a public vindication, since, in the

old days of quarrel, he had been legislated
out of his place in the House of Representatives; and, for the first and only time in my
life, I undertook to philosophize some comfort
for him—out of the fact that to the position
of authority which he held in Utah a Senatorship was a descent. He replied dryly: "I
understand, my son—perfectly." The fact
was that he needed no comfort from me or
any other human being. He seemed all-
sufficient to himself, because of the abiding
sense he had of the constant presence of God
and his habit of communing with that Spirit,
instead of seeking human intercourse or
earthly counsel. He did not need my affection. He did not need, much less seek, the
approbation of any man. In the events to
which this conversation was a prelude, he
acted without explaining himself to me or to
anyone else, and apparently without caring
in the slightest what my opinion or any other
man's might be of his course or of the motives
that prompted it.

Some months later, in the office of the
Presidency (at a business meeting with him,
Colonel Clayton and Joseph F. Smith), I ex-
cused myself from attending any further
sittings of the committee for that day, because I had to go to Provo to receive the Republican nomination for Congress.

My father said: "I am sorry to hear it.
I thought Judge Zane—or someone else—

would be nominated. I wished you to be free to help with these business matters. Why have you not consulted us?"

I reminded him that I had told him, some weeks before, that I expected to be nominated for Congress this year—and that I was practically certain, if elected, of going to the Senate when we were granted statehood. "I talked with you, then, as my father," I said. "But I'm sure you'll remember that I have not consulted you as a leader of the Church, or any of your colleagues as leaders of the Church, on the subject of partisan politics since the People's Party was dissolved."

He accepted this mild declaration of political independence without protest, and I went to Provo, happily, a free man. The Republicans nominated me by acclamation, and the chairman of the committee that came to offer me the nomination was Colonel Wm. Nelson, then managing editor of the *Salt Lake Tribune*, a Gentile, a former leader of the Liberal Party, an opponent of Mormonism as practised, who had fought the Church hierarchy for years. Here was a new evidence that we were now beyond the old quarrels—a further guarantee that we were prepared to take our place among the states of the Union, free of parochialism and its sectarian enmities.

The campaign gave every proof of such

political emancipation. The people divided,
on national party lines, as completely as any
American community in my experience.
The Democrats, having nominated Joseph
L. Rawlins, had the prestige that he had
gained in helping to pass the Enabling Act;
a Democratic administration was in power
in Washington; Apostle Moses Thatcher,
Brigham H. Roberts, and other members of
the Church inspired the old loyalty of the
Mormons for the Democracy. But the Republicans had been re-enforced by the dissolution
of the Liberal Party, whose last preceding
candidate (Mr. Clarence E. Allen) went on
the stump for us. The Smith jealousy of
Moses Thatcher divided the Church influence;
and though charges of ecclesiastical interference were made on both sides, such interference was personal rather than official.
Mr. Rawlins was defeated, and I was elected
delegate in Congress from the territory—
with the United States Senatorship practically assured to me.

In the spring of 1895 the constitutional
convention at Salt Lake City formulated a
provisional constitution for the new Utah;
and, in the Fall of the year, a general election
was held to adopt this constitution and to
elect officers who should enter upon their
duties as soon as Utah became a state. The
election was marked by a most significant
and important incident.

The Democrats, in their convention, nominated for Congress, Brigham H. Roberts, one of the first seven "presidents of the seventy," and for the United States Senate, Joseph L. Rawlins and Apostle Moses Thatcher. Immediately, at a priesthood meeting of the hierarchy, Joseph F. Smith denounced the candidacies of Roberts and Thatcher; and the grounds for the denunciation were subsequently stated in the "political manifesto" of April, 1896, in which the First Presidency announced, as a rule of the Church, that no official of the Church should accept a political nomination until he had obtained the permission of the Church authorities and had learned from them whether he could "consistently with the obligations already entered into with the Church, take upon himself the added duties and labors and responsibilities of the new position."

This action, I knew, was the result of the old jealousy of Thatcher which the Smiths had so long nursed. But it was also in line with the Church's pledge, to keep its leaders out of politics. By it, the hierarchy bound themselves and set the people free. The leaders, thereafter, according to their own "manifesto," could not enter politics without the consent of their quorums; and, therefore, by any American doctrine, they could not enter politics at all. Thatcher and Roberts revolted against the inhibition as an infringement of their rights as citizens, and it was so construed by the whole Democratic party; but everyone knew that a Mormon apostle had no rights as a citizen that were not second to his Church allegiance, and the political manifesto simply made public the fact of such subservience, authoritatively. We Republicans welcomed it, with our eyes on the future freedom of politics in Utah; Thatcher and Roberts refused to accept the dictation of their quorums, and what was practically an "edict of apostasy" went out against them. They were defeated. The Republican candidates (Heber M. Wells, as governor, and Clarence E. Allen, as member of Congress) were elected. Thatcher, subsequently refusing to accept the "political manifesto," was deposed from his apostolic authority, and deprived of all priesthood in the Church. Roberts recanted and was reconciled with the hierarchy.*

The Republicans elected forty-three out of sixty-three members of the legislature, and everyone of these had been pledged to support me, for the United States Senate, either by his convention, or by letter to me, or by a promise conveyed to me by friends; and none of these pledges had I solicited.

The rumors of my father's candidacy now became more general—although he was a

---

*He was afterwards elected to the House of Representatives and was refused his seat as a polygamist.

Democrat, although the new "political manifesto" bound him, although it was doubtful
whether the Senate would allow him to be
seated. Two influences were urging his election. One was the desire of the Smith faction
to have the First Councillor break the ice at
Washington for Apostle John Henry Smith,
who was ambitious to be a Senator and was
disqualified by the fact that he was a Church
leader and a polygamist. The other was the
desire of some Eastern capitalists to have my
father's vote in the Senate to aid them in the
promotion of a railroad from Salt Lake City
to Los Angeles. A preliminary agreement
for the construction of the road had already
been signed by men who represented that
they had close affiliations with large steel
interests in the East, as one party, and my
father as business representative of a group
of associates, including the Presidency of the
Church. The Church's interest in the project
was communistic, and so was my father's.
But his vote and influence in the Senate would
be valuable to the promotion of the undertaking, and he had received written assurances
from Republican leaders, senators and politicians, that if he were elected he would be
allowed his seat.

As a result of our Republican success in
the two political campaigns that had just
ended, I felt that I represented the independ-
ent votes of both Mormons and Gentiles;

and I decided to confront the First Presidency (as such a representative) and try to make them declare themselves in the matter of my father's candidacy. Not that I thought his candidacy would be so vitally important—for I did not then believe the Church authorities had power to sway the legislature away from its pledges. But every day, at home or abroad, I was being asked: "Are you *sure* that the Church's retirement from politics is sincere?" My friends were accepting my word, and I wished to add certainty to assurance that the Church leaders intended to fulfil the covenant of their personal honor and respect the constitution of the state by keeping out of politics.

Without letting them know why I wished to see them, I procured an appointment for the interview. When we were all seated at the table I explained: "I'm going to Washington to attend to my duties as delegate in Congress. Before I return, Utah will be admitted to statehood, and the legislature will have to elect two United States Senators. As you all know, I've been a candidate for one of these places. It has been assured to me by the probably unanimous vote of the Republican caucus when it shall convene." I laid my clenched hand on the table, knuckles down, with a calculated abruptness. "The first senatorship from Utah is *there*," I said. "If it's to be disturbed by any ecclesiastical direction, I want to know it *now*, so that the men who are supporting me may be aware of what they must encounter if they persist in their support. I ask you, as the Presidency of the Church: what are you going to do about the Senatorship?" And I opened my hand and left it lying open before them, for their decision.

It was evident enough, from their expressions, that this was a degree of boldness to which they were unaccustomed. It was evident also that they were unprepared to reply to me. My father remained silent, with his usual placidity, waiting for the others to fail to take the initiative. President Woodruff blinked, somewhat bewildered, looking at my hand as if the sight of its emptiness and the assumption of what it held, confused him. Joseph F. Smith, frowning, eyed it askance with a darting glance, apparently annoyed by the mute insolence of its demand for a decision which he was not prepared to make.

My father, at length, looking at me imperturbably, asked: "Are you inquiring of our personal view in this matter, Frank?"

The question contained, of course, a tacit allusion to my refusal to consult the Church leaders about politics. I answered: "No, sir. I already have *your* personal view. That is the only personal view I have ever asked concerning the Senatorship. And I have purposely refrained from any allusions to it of late, with you, because I wished to lay it before the Presidency, as a body, formally, in order that there might be no possible misunderstanding."

"In that case," he said, "the matter rests with President Woodruff."

The President, thus forced to an explanation, made a very characteristic one. Several of the Church's friends in the East, he said, had urged father's name for the Senatorship, but it was impossible to see how he could be spared from the affairs of the priesthood. Zion needed him—and so forth.

Apparently, to President Woodruff, the question of the Senatorship was resolvable wholly upon Church considerations. His mind was so filled with zealous hope for the advancement of "the Kingdom of God on Earth," that he seemed quite unaware of the political aspects of the case, the violation of the Church's pledge, and the difficulties in the Senate that would surely attend upon my father's election.

In the general discussion that ensued, both Joseph F. Smith and my father spoke of the appeal that had been made to them on behalf of the business interests of the community, with which the financial interests of the East were now eager to co-operate. But both followed the President's example in dismissing the possibility of the First Councillor's candidacy as infringing upon his duties in the

Church. I pointed out to them that such a candidacy would be considered a breach of faith, that it would raise a storm of protest. They accepted the warning without comment, as if, having decided against the candidacy, they did not need to consider such aspects of it. I kept my hand open before them until my father said, with some trace of amusement: "You'd better take up that senatorship, Frank. I think you're entitled to it."

I took it up, satisfied that there would be no more Church interference in the matter. The decision seemed to me final and momentous. I felt that the new Utah had faced the old and had been assured of independence.

About this same time (although I cannot place it accurately in my recollection), President Woodruff, speaking from the pulpit, declared that it was the right of the priesthood of God to rule in all things on earth, and that they had in no wise relinquished any of their authority. The sermon raised a dangerous alarm in Salt Lake City, and I was immediately summoned from Ogden (by a messenger from Church headquarters) to see the proprietor and the editor of the *Salt Lake Tribune*—which paper, it was feared, might oppose Utah's admission to statehood, construing President Woodruff's remarks to mean that the Church's political covenants were to be broken.

I found Mr. P. H. Lannan, the proprietor

of the paper, anxious, indignant and ready to denounce the Church and fight against the admission to statehood. "When I heard of that sermon," he said, "my heart went into my boots. We Gentiles have trusted everything to the promises that have been made by the leaders of the Church. If the *Tribune* had not supported the movement for statehood, the Gentiles would never have taken the risk. I feel like a man who has sold his brethren into slavery."

I assured him (as I was authorized to do) that President Woodruff was not speaking for our generation of the Mormon people nor for his associates in the leadership of the Church. I pleaded that it was the privilege of an old man (and President Woodruff was nearly ninety) to dream again the visions of his youth; his early life had been spent in the belief that a Kingdom of God was to be set up in the valleys of the mountains, governed by the priesthood and destined to rule all the nations of the earth; he had planted the first flag of the country over the Salt Lake Valley; he was still living in days that had passed for all but him, and cherishing hopes that he alone had not abandoned. But if the *Tribune* and the Gentiles would be magnanimous in this matter, they would add to the gratitude that already bound the younger generations of the Church to the fulfilment of its political promises.

Mr. Lannan responded instantly to the appeal to his generosity, and after consultation with the editor-in-chief (Judge C. C. Goodwin) and the managing editor (Colonel Wm. Nelson) the *Tribune* continued to trust in Mormon good faith.

I reported the result of my conference to Church headquarters. The news was received with relief and gratitude. And, in a long conversation with the authorities, I was told that it would be incumbent on us of the younger generation to see that all the Church's covenants to the nation should be scrupulously observed.

I accepted my part of the charge with a light heart, and late in November, 1895, I took train for Washington for convening of Congress. Of the incidents of my brief services as delegate I shall write nothing here, since those incidents were merely introductory to matters which I shall have to consider later. But I was greeted with a great deal of cordiality by the Republicans who credited me with having brought a state and its national representation into the Republican party, and they assured me that my own political future would be as bright as that of my native state!

President Cleveland, on January 4, 1896, proclaimed Utah a sovereign state of the Union, and its admission to statehood ended, of course, my service as a territorial delegate.

I stood beside his desk in the White House to see him sign the proclamation—the same desk at which he had received me, some eight years before, when I came beseeching him to be merciful to the proscribed people whose freedom he was now announcing. Perhaps the manumission that he was granting, gave a benignity to his face. Perhaps the emotion in my own mind transfigured him to me. But I saw smiles and pathos in the ruggedness of his expression of congratulation as he said a few words of hope that Utah would fulfil every promise made, on her behalf, by her own people, and every happy expectation that had been entertained for her by her friends. His enormous rigid bulk, a little bowed now by years of service, seemed softened, as his face was, to the graciousness of clement power. He gave me the pen with which he had signed the paper, and dismissed me to some of the happiest hours of my life.

I walked out of the White House dispossessed of office, but now, at last, a citizen of the Republic. I stood on the steps of the White House, to look at the city through whose streets I had so many times wandered in a worried despair, and I saw them with an emotion I would not dare transcribe. I do not know that the sun was really shining, but in my memory the scene has taken on all the accumulated brightnesses of all the radiant days I ever knew in Washington. And I remember that I saw the Washington Monument and the Capitol with a sense of almost affectionate *personal* possession!

In an excited exultation I went to thank the men who had helped us in the House and the Senate—to wire jubilant messages home—to send Governor Wells the pen with which the President had signed his proclamation, and to procure from friends in the War Department the first two flags that had been made with forty-five stars—the star of Utah the forty-fifth. Wherever I went, some sinister aspect seemed to have gone out of things; and I remember that I enjoyed so much the sense of their new inhostility, that I planned to delay my return to Utah until I had made a pilgrimage to every spot in Washington where I had despaired of our future.

All this may seem almost sentimental to you, who perhaps accept your citizenship as an unregarded commonplace of natural right. But, for me, the freeing of our people was an emancipation to be compared only to the enfranchisement of the Southern slaves—and greater even than *that*, for we had come from citizenship in the older states, and we could appreciate our deprivation, smart under our ostracism, and resent the rejection that set us apart from the rest of the nation as an inferior people unfit for equal rights.

I sat down to my dinner, that evening, with the appetite that comes from a day of fasting and emotional excitement; and I recall that I was planning a visit of self-congratulation to Arlington, for the morrow, when one of the hotel bell-boys brought me a telegram. I opened it eagerly—to enjoy the expected message of felicitation from home.

It was in cipher, and that fact gave me a pause of doubt, since the days of political mysteries and their cipher telegrams were over for us, thank God! It was signed with President Woodruff's cipher name.

I went to my room to translate it, and I did not return to my dinner. The message read: "It is the will of the Lord that your father shall be elected Senator from Utah."

I do not need to explain all the treacherous implications of that announcement. As soon as I had recovered my breath, I wired back, for such interpretation as they should choose to give: "God bless Utah. I am coming home,"—and packed my trunk, for trouble.

CHAPTER VII

THE FIRST BETRAYALS

Before I reached Utah, my friends, Ben Rich and James Devine, met me, on the train. The news of President Woodruff's "revelation" had percolated through the whole community. The Gentiles were alarmed for themselves. My friends were anxious for me. All the old enmities that had so long divided Utah were arranging themselves for a new conflict. And Rich and Devine had come to urge me to remember my promise that I would hold to my candidacy no matter who should appear in the field against me.

Of my father's stand in the crisis Rich could give me only one indication: after a conference in the offices of the Presidency, Rich had said to President Woodruff: "Then I suppose I may as well close up Frank's rooms at the Templeton"—the hotel in which my friends had opened political headquarters for me—and my father, accompanying him to an anteroom, had hinted significantly: "I think you should not close Frank's rooms just yet. He may need them."

Rich brought me word, too, that the Church authorities were expect'ng to see me; and as soon as I arrived in Salt Lake City, I hastened to the little plastered house in which the Presidency had its offices.

President Woodruff, my father, and Joseph F. Smith were there, in the large room of their official apartments. We withdrew, for private conference, into the small retiring room in which I had consulted with "Brother Joseph Mack" when he was on the underground— in 1888—and had consulted with President Woodruff about his "manifesto," in 1890. The change in their circumstances, since those unhappy days, was in my mind as I sat down.

President Woodruff sat at the head of a bare walnut table in a chair so large that it rather dwarfed him; and he sank down in it, to an attitude of nervous reluctance to speak, occupied with his hands. Smith took his place at the opposite end of the board, with dropped eyes, his chair tilted back, silent, but (as I soon saw) unusually alert and attentive. My father assumed his inevitable composure—firmly and almost unmovingly seated—and looked at me squarely with a not unkind premonition of a smile.

President Woodruff continued silent. Ordinarily, anything that came from the Lord was quite convincing to him and needed no argument (in his mind) to make it convincing to others. I could not suppose that the look of determination on my face troubled him. It was more likely that something unusual in the mental attitudes of his councillors was

the cause of his hesitation; and with this
suspicion to arouse me I became increasingly
aware (as the conference proceeded) of two
rival watchfulnesses upon me.

"Well?" I said. "What was it you wanted
of me?"

Smith looked up at the President. And
Smith had always, hitherto, seemed so un-
seeing of consequences, and, therefore, un-
appreciative of means, that his betrayal of
interest was indicative of purpose. I thought
I could detect, in the communication which
his manner made, the plan of my father's
ecclesiastical rivals to remove him from the
scene of his supreme influence over the President, and the plan of ambitious church politicians to remove me from their path by the
invocation of God's word appointing father
to the Senate.

"Frank," the President announced, "it
is the will of the Lord that your father should
go to the Senate from Utah."

As he hesitated, I said: "Well, President
Woodruff?"

He added, with less decision: "And we
want you to tell us how to bring it about?"

It was evident that getting the revelation
was easy to his spiritualized mind, but that
fulfilling it was difficult to his unworldliness.

"President Woodruff," I replied, "you
have received the revelation on the wrong
point. You do not need a voice from heaven

161

to convince anyone that my father is worthy to go to the Senate, but you will need a revelation to tell how he is to get there."

He seemed to raise himself to the inspiration of divine authority. "The only difficulty that we have encountered," he said, "is the fact that the legislators are pledged to you. Will you not release them from their promises and tell them to vote for your father?"

"No," I said. "And my father would not permit me to do it, even if I could. He knows that I gave my word of honor to my supporters to stand as a candidate, no matter who might enter against me. He knows that he and I have given our pledges at Washington that political dictation in Utah by the heads of the Mormon Church shall cease. Of all men in Utah *we* cannot be amenable to such dictation. If you can get my supporters away from me—very well. I shall have no personal regrets. But you cannot get me away from my supporters."

This inclusion of my father in my refusal evidently disconcerted President Woodruff; and, as evidently, it had its significance to Joseph F. Smith.

I went on: "Before I was elected to the House of Representatives, I asked my father if he intended to be a candidate for the Senate. I knew that some prominent Gentiles, desiring to curry favor at Church headquarters had solicited his candidacy. I had been told

shoulders. "This boy," he said, "is acting honorably. I want him to know—and you to know—that I respect the position he has taken. If he is elected, he shall have my blessing."

That was the only understanding I had with him—but it was enough. I could know that I was not to lose his trust and affection by holding to our obligations of honor; and—an assurance almost as precious—I could know that he would not consciously permit legislators to be crushed by the vengeance of the Church if they refused to yield to its pressure.

A few days after my arrival in Utah, and while this controversy was at its height, my father's birthday was celebrated (January 11, 1896), with all the patriarchal pomp of a Mormon family gathering, in his big country house outside Salt Lake City. All his descendants and collateral relatives were there, as well as the members of the Presidency and many friends. After dinner, the usual exercises of the occasion were held in the large reception hall of the house, with President Woodruff and my father and two or three other Church leaders seated in semi-state at one end of the hall, and the others of the company deferentially withdrawn to face them. Towards the end of the programme President Woodruff rose from his easy chair, and made a sort of informal address of congratulation; and in the course of it, with his

hand on my father's shoulder, he said be-
nignly: "Abraham was the friend of God.
He had only one son on whom all his hopes
were set. But the voice of the Lord commanded him to sacrifice Isaac upon an altar;
and Abraham trusted the Lord and laid his
son upon the altar, in obedience to God's
commands. Now here is another servant
of the Most High and a friend of God. I
refer to President Cannon, whose birthday
we are celebrating. He has twenty-one sons;
and if it shall be the will of the Lord that he
must sacrifice one of them he ought to be as
willing as Abraham was, for he will have
twenty left. And the son should be as willing
as Isaac. We can all safely trust in the Lord.
He will require no sacrifice at our hands without purpose."

I remarked to a relative beside me that
the altar was evidently ready for me, but that
I feared I should have to "get out and rustle
my own ram in the thicket." I received no
reply. I heard no word of comment from
anyone upon the President's speech. It was
accepted devoutly, with no feeling that he
had abused the privileges of a guest. Everyone understood (as I did) that President
Woodruff was the gentlest of men; that he
had often professed and always shown a
kindly affection for me; but that the will of
the Lord being now known, he thought I
should be *proud* to be sacrificed to it!

Among the legislators pledged to me were Mormon Bishops and other ecclesiasts who had promised their constituents to vote for me and who now stood between a betrayal of their people and a rebellion against the power of the hierarchy. I released one of them from his pledge, because of his pathetic fear that he would be eternally damned if he did not obey "the will of the Lord." The others went to the Presidency to admit that if they betrayed their people they would have to confess what pressure had been put upon them to force them to the betrayal. I went to notify my father (as I had notified the representatives of every other candidate) that we were going to call a caucus of the Republican majority of the legislature, and later I was advised that President Woodruff and his Councillors had appointed a committee to investigate and report to them how many members could be counted upon to support my father's candidacy. The committee (composed of my uncle Angus, my brother Abraham, and Apostle John Henry Smith) brought back word that even among the men who had professed a willingness to vote for my father there was great reluctance and apprehension, and that in all probability his election could not be carried. With President Woodruff's consent, my father then announced that he was not a candidate. I was nominated by acclamation.

When I called upon my father at the President's offices after the election, he said to me before his colleagues: "I wish to congratulate you on having acted honorably and fearlessly. You have my blessing." He turned to the President. "You see, President Woodruff," he added, "it was not the will of the Lord, after all, since the people did not desire my election!"

I have dwelt so largely upon the religious aspects of this affair because they are as true of the Prophet in politics today as they were then. At the time, the personal complication of the situation most distressed me—the fact that I was opposing my father in order to fulfil the word of honor that we had given on behalf of the Mormon leaders. But there was another view of the matter; and it is the one that is most important to the purposes of this narrative. In the course of the various discussions and conferences upon the Senatorship, I learned that the inspiration of the whole attempted betrayal had come from certain Republican politicians and lobbyists (like Colonel Isaac Trumbo), who claimed to represent a political combination of business interests in Washington. Joseph F. Smith admitted as much to me in more than one conversation. (I had offended these interests by opposing a monetary and a tariff bill during my service as delegate in Congress—a matter which I have still to recount). They had chosen my father and Colonel Trumbo as Utah's two Senators. I made it my particular business to see that Trumbo's name was not even mentioned in the caucus. The man selected as the other senator was Arthur Brown, a prominent Gentile lawyer who was known as a "jack-Mormon" (meaning a Gentile adherent to Church power), although I then believed, and do now, that Judge Chas. C. Goodwin was the Gentile most entitled to the place, because of his ability and the love of his people.

I was, however, content with the victory we had won by resisting the influence of the business interests that had been willing to sell our honor for their profit, and I set out for Washington with a determination to continue the resistance. I was in a good position to continue it. The election of two Republican Senators from Utah had given the Republicans a scant majority of the members of the Upper House, and the bills that I had fought in the Lower House were now before the Senate.

These bills had been introduced in the House of Representatives, immediately upon its convening in December, 1895, by the committee on rules, before Speaker Reed had even appointed the general committees. One was a bill to authorize the issuance of interest-bearing securities of the United States at such times and in such sums as the Executive might determine. The other was a general tariff bill that proposed increases upon the then existing Wilson-Gorman bill. The first would put into the hands of the President a power that was not enjoyed by any ruler in Christendom; the second would add to the unfair and discriminatory tariff rates then in force, by making *ad valorem* increases in them. Many new members of Congress had been elected on the two issues thus created: the arbitrary increase of the bonded indebtedness by President Cleveland to maintain a gold reserve; and the unjust benefits afforded those industries that were least in need of aid, by duties increased in exact proportion to the strength of the industrial combination that was to be protected.

The presentation of the two bills by the Committee on Rules—with a coacher to each proposing to prevent amendment and limit discussion—raised a revolt in the House. A caucus of the insurgent Republican members was held at the Ebbitt Hotel, and I was elected temporary chairman. We appointed a committee to demand from Speaker Reed a division of the questions and time for opposition to be heard. We had seventy-five insurgents when our committee waited on Reed; and most of us were new men, elected to oppose such measures as these bills advocated. He received us with sarcasm, put us off with a promise to consider our demands, and then set his lieutenants at work among us. Under the threat of the Speaker's displeasure if we continued to "insurge" and the promise of his favor if we "got into line," forty-one (I think) of our seventy-five deserted us. We were gloriously beaten in the House on both measures.

Some of the older Republican members of the House came to ask me how I had been "misled"; and they received with the raised eyebrow and the silent shrug my explanation that I had been merely following my convictions and living up to the promises I had made my constituents. I had supposed that I was upholding an orthodox Republican doctrine in helping to defend the country from exploitation by the financial interests, in the matter of the bond issue, and from the greed of the business interests in the attempt to increase horizontally the tariff rates.

I do not need, in this day of tariff reform agitation, to argue the injustice of the latter measure. But the bond issue—looking back upon it now—seems the more cruelly absurd of the two. Here we were, in times of peace, with ample funds in the national treasury, proposing to permit the unlimited issuance of interest-bearing government bonds in order to procure gold, for that national treasury, out of the hoards of the banks, so that these same banks might be able to obtain the gold

171

again from the treasury in return for paper money. The extent to which this sort of absurdity might be carried would depend solely upon the desire of the confederation of finance to have interest-bearing government bonds on which they might issue national bank notes, since the Executive was apparently willing to yield interminably to their greed, in the belief that he was protecting the public credit by encouraging the financiers to attack that credit with their raids on the government gold reserve. The whole difficulty had arisen, of course, out of the agitation upon the money question. The banks were drawing upon the government gold reserve; and the government was issuing bonds to recover the gold again from the banks.

I had been, for some years, interested in the problem of our monetary system and had studied and discussed it among our Eastern bankers and abroad. The very fact that I was from a "silver state" had put me on my guard, lest a local influence should lead me into economic error. I had grown into the belief that our system was wrong. It seemed to me that some remedy was imperative. I saw in bimetallism a part of the remedy, and I supported bimetallism not as a partisan of free coinage but as an advocate of monetary reform.

The arrival of Utah's two representatives

in the Senate (January 27, 1896) gave the
bimetallists a majority, and when the bond-
issue bill came before us we made it into a
bill to permit the free coinage of silver.
(February 1). A few days later, the Finance
Committee turned the tariff bill into a free-
coinage bill also. On both measures, five
Republican Senators voted against their
party—Henry M. Teller, of Colorado; Fred
T. Dubois, of Idaho; Thos. H. Carter, of
Montana; Lee Mantle, of Montana; and
myself. We were subsequently joined by
Richard F. Pettigrew of South Dakota.
Within two weeks of my taking the oath in
the Senate we were read out of the party
by Republican leaders and Republican organs.

All this happened so swiftly that there was
no time for any remonstrances to come to me
from Salt Lake City, even if the Church authorities had wished to remonstrate. The fact
was that the people of Utah were with us in
our insurgency, and when the financial interests subsequently appealed to the hierarchy,
they found the Church powerless to aid them
in support of a gold platform. But they
obtained that aid, at last, in support of a
tariff that was as unjust to the people as it
was favorable to the trusts, and my continued
"insurgency" led me again into a revolt
against Church interference.

The thread of connection that ran through
these incidents is clear enough to me now:

they were all incidents in the progress of a partnership between the Church and the predatory business interests that have since so successfully exploited the country. But, at the time, I saw no such connection clearly. I supposed that the partnership was merely a political friendship between the Smith faction in the Church and the Republican politicians who wished to use the Church; and I had sufficient contempt for the political abilities of the Smiths to regard their conspiracy rather lightly.

Believing still in the good faith of the Mormon people and their real leaders in authority, I introduced a joint resolution in the Senate restoring to the Church its escheated real estate, which was still in the hands of a receiver, although its personal property had been already restored. In conference with Senators Hoar and Allison,—of the committee to which the resolution was referred—I urged an unconditional restoration of the property, arguing that to place conditions upon the restoration would be to insult the people who had given so many proofs of their willingness to obey the law and keep their pledges. The property was restored without conditions by a joint resolution that passed the Senate on March 18, 1896, passed the House a week later, and was approved by the President on March 26. The Church was now free of the last measure of proscription. Its people were

174